Days of the Jungle

Days of the Jungle

DAYS
of the
JUNGLE

The Testimony of a Guatemalan *Guerrillero*, 1972-1976

by Mario Payeras

Introduction by George Black

Monthly Review Press

Copyright © 1983 by Monthly Review Press

All rights reserved

Originally published as *Los días de la selva*
by Casa de las Américas, Havana, Cuba

Library of Congress Catalogue Card Number: 83-13248

ISBN 0-85345-648-8

Monthly Review Press
155 West 23rd Street
New York, N.Y. 10011

Manufactured in the United States of America

10 9 8 7 6 5 4 3 2 1

Introduction:
Guatemala's Silent War

George Black

In the clamor of debate surrounding the crisis in Central America, there is a strange silence. It concerns Guatemala. Guatemala, with 7.2 million people, is the most populous country in the isthmus; it has the region's largest economy. Yet when President Ronald Reagan, for instance, took the unusual step of addressing a joint session of Congress on April 27, 1983, to seek support for his confrontational policies in Central America, Guatemala was all but absent. The key country in the region merited just two mentions in Reagan's speech, both of them cursory.

What fundamentally determines the level of public debate is of course the degree of direct U.S. involvement. Since Congress placed Guatemala on a list of gross human rights violators in 1977, making it ineligible for military or nonessential economic aid, that involvement has been subtle, cautious, and—where necessary—covert. Washington, in the parlance of policy-making, has little "leverage" over Guatemala's defiant pariah regime, and for six years has kept a nervous and watchful distance.

A higher imperative than qualms about human rights violations, however, is that the United States has not *needed* to become directly enmeshed in Guatemalan politics in recent years. It will do so only if the fragile foreign policy equation—balanc-

3

ing "threatened national interest" against "acceptable political cost"—appears to discount all other options. That moment came once in 1954; it came again in 1967-68. The first time the CIA did the job, overthrowing the duly elected reformist government of Jacobo Arbenz; the second time it fell to the Green Berets, who helped the local army mop up a powerful guerrilla movement. Since then the Guatemalan armed forces, built up under U.S. tutelage to become the most efficient killing force in the region, have largely kept control. This is a professional and highly technified army, designed for counterinsurgency; it is not a "nineteenth-century constabulary," as a U.S. official once derisively characterized its Salvadorean counterpart.

So far Guatemala's revolutionaries have not taken state power, as they have in Nicaragua. Nor, despite their rash optimism, which followed on the heels of the Sandinista triumph, do they immediately threaten to do so. Furthermore, the Central American quagmire has shown the United States since 1980 just how high the political cost of even inconclusive intervention can be. For both reasons, the U.S. Right prefers for the moment to keep its counsel over Guatemala.

Even so, the omission of Guatemala from public debate remains a curious one, especially when we consider the terms in which the regional polemic is phrased. From the Right, there is the constant insistence on a bipolar world vision to drag Central America screaming into the arena of power bloc hostilities; from the Left, an equally impassioned counter-thrust that the revolutionary challenge confronting Washington and its regional client regimes is a purely indigenous phenomenon. On both counts, Guatemala embodies the stakes of the regional crisis much more completely than do the smaller states of El Salvador and Nicaragua.

For the moment, it may appear that El Salvador is the place for drawing lines of containment. That is where the rhetorical posturing of the administration has taken us, ever since the day in early 1981 when Secretary of State Alexander Haig determined that tiny, "manageable" El Salvador was a convenient low-risk setting for making grand Cold War gestures, appealing precisely *because* the country lacked any intrinsic strategic importance and held out no attraction for large-scale

Soviet involvement. For the moment, then, the brutalities of un-mediated class warfare in Guatemala pass almost unnoticed. The massacre and displacement of entire highland Indian com-munities, and the rampages of urban death-squads against re-formist politicians, are journalistic curiosities, like Costa Rica's foreign debt or Belize's independence. Briefly, they spark a few column inches, but they are essentially anomalous, unrelated to the "real" regional crisis being played out in El Salvador and Nicaragua.

Nevertheless, it is in Guatemala that the decisive battles for the future of Central America will be fought; and the sheer human cost will surely surpass anything we have yet seen—after all, the Guatemalan opposition will tell anyone willing to listen that 85,000 people have already died in political violence since 1954. And it is in Guatemala that the eventual direct in-volvement of U.S. ground combat forces is most probable—just as it proved necessary to send in the Green Berets during the 1960s.

Already Washington is ensnared in a war it cannot win in El Salvador. The same logic will make the Guatemalan war—when it finally emerges into the light—even more unwinnable. The fact that the local military is out of control is one factor. So too is the absence of a credible political center on which to pin the threadbare Kirkpatrick fantasy of democratizing the authori-tarian Right. In Guatemala even more than El Salvador, the center has withered and died. In part, it has been deemed re-dundant within the controlled political schema allowed by the military. And in part, it has been physically exterminated—not least to head off any danger that it might one day present a realistic option for U.S. support. Washington, in a word, is stuck with the monster it has done so much to create.

Measured in importance by the standard strategic indica-tors of the Pentagon and State Department—its size, location, and possession of raw materials—Guatemala beats El Salvador hands down as a place for the Free World to make a stand. It shares a long and practically indefensible land border with Mexi-co; that border backs on to Mexico's vast southern oilfields; and Guatemala has oil deposits of its own, even though they may not be as great as once touted, as well as rich nickel deposits along the shores of Lake Izabal. Pentagon planners speak of it as the contingency site for a regional military base, a staging-post for troops based in the Panama Canal Zone. On the economic front, direct U.S. investments, at some $260 million, are the highest in the region, and such corporate giants as Exxon, IBM, Texaco, and ITT have taken root in Guatemala as they never did in El Salvador or Nicaragua.

These investments did not arrive out of the blue. Like the counterinsurgency state, they are there because Guatemala was once before rescued from communism and made safe for Western Christian Civilization. El Salvador and Nicaragua were foreign policy backwaters; Guatemala was a fully fledged regional guinea pig for investment, development, and antiguerrilla strategies. It will not be Ronald Reagan who thrusts Guatemala on to the East-West chessboard; it has been there since 1964, when the CIA installed a sleazy dictator named Colonel Carlos Castillo Armas in the National Palace. The fact is that Guatemala's current festering crisis is the child of the first Cold War. Indeed, along with Iran and Greece, Guatemala provides a cardinal definition of what the Cold War was all about. Reagan's explicit resurrection of the Truman Doctrine to legitimize present policies leaves little doubt that the renewed defense of Guatemala will again be considered ineluctable.

If the U.S. Right is correct in claiming Guatemala as a superpower issue, the Left's insistence that it is a purely domestic matter is, paradoxically, even more justified. A recent book makes the point eloquently: it calls the Guatemalan revolution "unfinished history."* In the years of the postwar economic boom, the United States demanded a new role from the fragile economies of Central America. The archaic coffee-based tyrannies of the day were not up to the task, and throughout the isthmus they were swept away by modernizers who spoke of economic diversification, industrialization—even reform. In Costa Rica, the result was electoral democracy, even a fledgling welfare state; in El Salvador, Nicaragua, and Honduras varied

---

* Jonathan L. Fried, Marvin E. Gettleman, Deborah T. Levenson, and Nancy Peckenham, eds., *Guatemala in Rebellion: Unfinished History* (New York: Grove Press, 1983).

forms of right-wing realignments. Nowhere, however, did the process run as deep as in the "revolutionary" process set in motion in Guatemala after 1944. Two successive governments not only confronted the local oligarchy and opened up the space for mass mobilization, but locked horns with the U.S. monopolies in the shape of the United Fruit Company. That of course, over and above any domestic contradictions of the reform process, any debate over the imminence of socialist transformation, proved their nemesis.

The violent uprooting of bourgeois democracy that resulted lies at the very heart of the Guatemalan revolution. It infuses the collective national consciousness even more deeply than the 1932 *matanza*—when 30,000 people were killed—does for Salvadoreans. Since 1954, Guatemalans have lived in a long darkness, in which the shades of gray have been nothing more than the nuances of counterrevolutionary violence. With no space to allow a legal opposition to regroup, the road to armed revolt has long seemed warranted—whether to disaffected military officers or nostalgic democrats, visionary socialists or marginalized Mayan Indians.

When the roots of revolt lie this deep, it is hard for even the most baleful of State Department propagandists to lay the blame for the insurgency at Cuba's door, and there has been little conviction in the lame attempts to do so. After all, when the Guatemalan revolution began, Fidel Castro was a sixteen-year-old basketball star at a Jesuit high school. The war being fought by Guatemala's revolutionaries is thus indigenous in two senses. Indigenous because, even more than in El Salvador or Nicaragua, these revolutionaries have honed their structures and ideology quite independent of Cuban or other foreign advice; and indigenous because, increasingly, the Indian majority have become the main protagonists of the war. That population, long dubbed passive and withdrawn by tourist promoters and leftist intellectuals alike, has cultivated silence as chameleon-cover for its ceaselessly inventive revolt against domination.

Now comes this long overdue book from Mario Payeras as a first break in that silence. His subject is the formative years of the first cadre of the Ejército Guerrillero de los Pobres (EGP)— the Guerrilla Army of the Poor—in the remote northwestern jungles of the Ixcán between 1972 and 1976. His style reminds us that though the content of guerrilla warfare is harsh and unromantic, the perceptions it generates may still be lyrical. And if lyricism seems a strange quality in a guerrilla leader, an unexpected companion to dialectical rigor, let the reader turn to a 1981 interview between Payeras and the Chilean writer Marta Harnecker for confirmation that a *guerrillero*'s motivation can be profoundly human. "What did the experience of the Ixcán teach you?" asks Harnecker. Among other things, replies Payeras, that "it was just as important to love the yellow flower of the *tamborillo* in February as it was to learn how to love and truly respect our *compañeros*."

Like any microscopic eyewitness report from a battlefront, the narrative that Payeras lays before us throws out elusive clues to the broader sweep of history surrounding it. The EGP's story speaks of military repression and the current government; it tantalizes us with mentions of political work in the cities, even an urban guerrilla front. Payeras does not demand an exhaustive glossary, but he begs a frame. What happened before this small band of men crossed the border from Mexico, and what has developed since the last page of the book was written? And beyond the suffocating jungle world of the Ixcán, how was the rest of Guatemala behaving between 1972 and 1976?

More than once, Payeras talks of his group as survivors, and refers to the Edgar Ibarra Front, hinting at a previous incarnation of guerrilla warfare in Guatemala. And that is another vital clue to the silence of the Guatemalan Left. For that earlier guerrilla movement had made its fatal mistakes in the full embarrassing glare of international publicity. Worse still, the subsequent self-criticism pointed to overeager self-publicizing as a reason for defeat in itself. "By the time they had given enough interviews," Régis Debray wrote caustically, "they came to believe the things they had heard on the best authority: their own."

In the 1960s the international press corps swarmed to be photographed next to real-live guerrillas with beards and bandoleros. They flocked to Venezuela, to Colombia, but most of all to Guatemala, for this was the most vibrant guerrilla movement since the Cuban revolution, and by 1966 it seemed set for an assault on state power. Yet within two years the movement that had captured world headlines was all but annihilated.

On the face of it, the reason was the aerial bombing, search-and-destroy missions, and napalm that devastated the eastern mountains, the guerrillas' chosen zone of operations. But the army's counterinsurgency campaign only hastened a process of political disintegration already underway inside the Left. The problems had been latent from the beginning. The roots of the movement lay in an abortive young officers' coup of November 1960, motivated by low army pay, corruption, and the blatant use of Guatemalan territory to train Cuban exiles for the Bay of Pigs invasion. Pardoned by a high command that refused— with that gentlemanliness peculiar to thugs—to punish its own kind, the young officers took to the mountains. Two of the more celebrated were Marco Antonio Yon Sosa and Luis Turcios Lima.

But military officers, however shrewdly they turn their Fort Bragg- and Fort Benning-acquired skills against an enemy, do not necessarily make the best political leaders for a burgeoning movement. That failure to mesh the political and the military aspects of the war bedeviled them from the outset, and explains much of the fierce internal rancor. The guerrillas of the 1960s, though never numbering more than 500, had neither a unified coherent political strategy nor a unified coherent organization that might have carried one out. The multiplying acronyms— FAR, MR-13, FGEI—were the visible token of this constant dilemma. One entrusted the political conduct of the war to a small cadre of Trotskyist advisers, and groped toward the chimera of instant socialist insurrection; one allowed the small local Communist Party to become the "brains" of the movement— for which they paid dearly, being treated as a kind of low-level pressure group that would hasten the equally chimerical bourgeois reform.

Beset by this startling degree of confusion about goals and methods, it was hardly surprising that these early guerrillas should fall prey to the worst excesses of *foquismo,* operating at the periphery of a population whose loyalty was indispensable. For their terrain they chose the eastern department of Izabal and the arid, scrubby hills of the Sierra de las Minas. The northwestern altiplano, today the principal theater of war, was all but ignored. Too many fell victim to the Communist Party's insistence that the Indian peasants of the altiplano—though more than half the population—were a "backward" force incapable of revolutionary initiative. In the east, among the ladino peasant population,* the guerrillas never overcame the taint of being outsiders, whatever spontaneous sympathy they generated—and that was real enough. Confident that spontaneity was a large part of victory, they allowed security lapses that today would appear laughable were they not so tragic. When the full weight of counterinsurgency struck the Sierra de las Minas, the guerrillas were pitifully unprepared to protect their civilian supporters, who accounted for the majority of the 8,000 body count.

The wisdom of hindsight shows the guerrillas as a tiny force operating on the margin of society. Yet in 1966 they were pressing the army hard in the military arena, and their political voice resonated far beyond their real organized strength. At the height of this influence that year, they were thrown off guard by that Guatemalan *rara avis,* the ostensibly clean presidential election. Civilian candidate Julio César Méndez Montenegro certainly acted and talked like a reformist. The question, though, that the Left fatally overlooked was whether the army would allow him to take power and enact a reformist program. He offered amnesty to the guerrillas, and they, although divided, in the end trusted in his good faith: a costly illusion, which succeeded only in demobilizing their supporters. The business-suited "reformist" candidate took office on schedule (Washington, ever adept during the Alliance for Progress at the art of the facade, saw to that). But not before the military had extracted its pound of flesh—an agreement from Méndez that real political power, along with carte blanche in the handling of the war, would be shifted from the National Palace to the barracks.

It was another step in the creeping monopoly of power by

---

* While the term ladino typically refers to those of mixed Indian and Spanish blood, Indians who have advanced their economic status or abandoned the visible symbols of their culture—costume, religious practices—may also consider themselves ladinos.

the armed forces. A 1963 coup, in many senses the ideological precursor of those which would sweep the Southern Cone in the name of national security during the 1970s, had set the tone. Then came a new constitution, in 1965, in which the armed forces dictated the narrow margins within which civilian politicians could play the electoral game. Finally, in 1967-68, the army took the defense of electoral democracy from Communist guerrillas as a convenient smokescreen for its own shift to the center of power. Its "Operation Guatemala" counterinsurgency drive crushed the Left, and left the army as sole effective arbiter of a process in which politics was defined as class war and all participation through institutional channels was progressively blocked off.

The new breed of army officers prided themselves not merely on being efficient fighting men, but technocrats and businessmen. Their doyen was General Carlos Arana Osorio, better known at the time as the "Butcher of Zacapa." In charge of antiguerrilla operations in 1968, within two years he was installed as president. For the military elite who managed the new political model, state power became a launching pad to wealth through agro-exporting, industry, finance, and real estate. The guardians of bourgeois wealth abruptly became Guatemala's leading economic force in their own right.

Days of the Jungle opens in 1972, a year and a half into Arana's presidency. By then the military appeared to have the country in a stranglehold. The bloodbath, they believed, had worked its magic and dismembered the resistance. But here the Guatemalan guerrillas—or politico-military organizations, the new term which crept into the lexicon in the 1970s—distinguish themselves from other contemporary Latin American movements. Annihilated at the zenith of its influence, the Guatemalan Left was to stage a major resurgence, based on a top-to-bottom analysis of its earlier failures. The tattered survivors of 1968 retreated and regrouped. To keep track of their movements, shifts, and alliances over the next four years is no easy matter, nor is it our task here.

The group in Payeras' account, remnants of the old Edgar Ibarra guerrilla front, had long questioned the wisdom of the foco theory and stressed the need for mass participation, particularly among the peasants. They now introduced a new term into the vocabulary—popular revolutionary war, a long, painstaking process that might take twenty years. It was these men who entered the jungles of the Ixcán to build a network of peasant support where the local structures of the state were at their most vulnerable. It is their story that is recounted in *Days of the Jungle*. This phase of "implantation" is how the prolonged war begins.

Of course, sixteen men in a nightmarish jungle environment, occupied as much with fighting off diarrhea and leeches as with forging a people's army from among the desperately poor slash-and-burn settlers of the region, are not going to make the revolution alone. Those who read Payeras' account with that illusion can only end by patronizing its endeavor. They will remain blind too to the long-range vision that breathes life into that endeavor, forgetting that in the talk of Latin American revolutionaries the metaphors of "seeds" and "germination" are central.

The Ixcán enterprise was one of a number of simultaneous arenas, and the EGP just one of a number of groups, in the revival of the movement. Those who survived the 1960s, and embraced its harsh lessons, grappled from the first with the thorniest of issues—how to unify the revolutionary forces. What this involves is, first, to come to terms with the special problems of three quite distinct geographical fronts—the largely Indian highlands, the rich agricultural belt of the south coast, and the cities. Then they must arduously carve unity from the dizzying mosaic of race, class, and ideology that characterizes modern Guatemala. The military-dominated political order excludes subsistence farmers, rural migrant laborers, and sharecroppers alike; it oppresses urban factory workers, marginal slumdwellers, and middle-class professionals. Each group presents its own experiences, its own susceptibilities, its own special problems. Ideologies too must be harmonized—traditional Marxism with liberation theology; the historic grievances of twenty-two ethnic groups of Mayan Indians with the rebellious rage of the long-term unemployed.

The EGP placed its greatest emphasis on the northwest

highlands, convinced that only through the combined resolution of class conflict and ethnic demands could the Guatemalan revolution acquire its special stamp. Others held out for a more urban-based approach. One group, the Fuerzas Armadas Rebeldes (FAR), or Rebel Armed Forces—inheritors of the name from the 1960s—reached that conclusion after a series of bitter reverses when it tried to reopen short-lived guerrilla fronts, most in the wilds of the Petén, the jungle department that sprawls northward to Mexico and Belize. By 1971 the FAR was ready to move into the factories of the capital and the vast plantations of the torrid south coast lowlands.

That shift drew them closer to the traditional Communist Partido Guatemalteco del Trabajo (PGT)—Guatemalan Workers' Party—with its strictly urban perspective. At the party's heated 1969 congress there had been a tepid verbal commitment to armed struggle and a long, multifaceted war, but in practice the PGT kept its distance from military work. Both the FAR and the PGT now set their sights on the distant goal of a mass-based working-class party; but the Communists in particular found that their insistence on sticking to semi-legal—and thus highly visible—work left them a sitting target for the security forces and death squads.

To others still, this *idée fixe* of urban work bordered on racism in multi-ethnic Guatemala. The FAR's western front, operating in the western Indian areas of Quezaltenango and San Marcos, took particular exception to the new line. In September 1971, while the EGP nucleus was readying its entrance from Mexico, the dissidents began independent work among the indigenous subsistence farmers of the western altiplano and the laborers of the piedmont. Only after eight years of silent preparations—during which not a single shot was fired—did they acknowledge their existence publicly, under the name of the Organización del Pueblo en Armas (ORPA)— Organization of the People in Arms.

Much of this theorizing stemmed from assumptions that the urban working-class movement was dead. Given the severity of the treatment meted out to the labor unions since 1954, and particularly the heavy repression of Arana's first months in power, the military's complacency seemed as reasonable as the

Left's despondency. But it would be a travesty of history to depict the Guatemalan struggle of the 1970s as an exclusively rural one. If anything, the opposite is true. While the EGP and its counterpart organizations remained active but mute, the front line—and the public fare—of political conflict pitched the labor unions against the military. Public schoolteachers, 20,000 of them, showed the way forward with a successful strike in 1973. Railroad, electricity, and tobacco workers followed their lead; eventually, from 1976 to 1980, the whole labor movement would confront the government.

The decade was one of long and arduous convergence between the urban and the rural, between one organization and another. It would take ten years to hammer out unitary agreements between the EGP, FAR, ORPA, and the PGT. The problems they faced were not peculiar to Guatemala. As in El Salvador, the move toward the unity of the Left is simultaneously apparent on three levels. While the leadership grapples with major theoretical stumbling blocks, the mass of their followers, more practical minded, may chafe with impatience and incomprehension. The most intractable are the middle-level cadre. Fiercely loyal to the group they have fought for, they are the most prone to the sectarian skirmishes and tunnel vision bred by an underground existence.

The year 1976 brings *Days of the Jungle* to a close. All the omens suggested that it would be a tranquil year. It was the second full year of the rule of General Kjell Laugerud, and he felt sufficiently in control of dissent to offer a limited opening up of Guatemala's political life. But, as is so often the case, lifting the lid only showed how fiercely the pot was boiling. In the wake of the catastrophic February earthquake, slumdwellers and churchpeople added their militant voice to the opposition. The resurgent labor movement came to maturity within a national umbrella organization. Resistance bred terror; terror bred fresh resistance—this was the dialectic of the 1970s.

Guatemala, according to popular wisdom, invented the death squad. As the decade wore on, the activities of these squads became grimly apparent: the mutilated corpses of those dragged away in unmarked Cherokee Chief stationwagons under cover of darkness began to turn up in storm drains and under bridges at a sickening rate—ten, fifteen, twenty a day. Labor, peasant, and student leaders were the main target. So were even moderate political figures, the very Christian Democrats and social democrats who had agreed to play the electoral game by the military's rules.

As the death squads ran wild under the successive regimes of Arana, Laugerud, and then Lucas García, the political schema drawn up by the military looked increasingly threadbare. One fraudulent election followed another, each more breathtaking in its flagrancy. By the time of the March 1978 "election," only a little over a third of registered voters even bothered to show up, and Lucas could lay claim to the support of a mere 8 percent of the adult population. The model that the army called "limited democracy" by now lay in tatters; the system began to unravel at the seams.

As the union movement was forced underground by the carnage and centrist politicians abandoned any hope of seeking peaceful change through the ballot box, the politico-military organizations of the Left began to appear to more and more Guatemalans as the only viable and broadly based alternative to the generals. The best recruiting agent for the Left was the continuing rule of the military. Businessmen, squeezed aside by the generals' gangster-like methods of competition, began to grumble that the country was being "Somozanized." Already excluded from the state, they found that the machinery of the free market served them little better.

Even the much-vaunted monolithic unity of the armed forces began to collapse, with hard-pressed field officers resenting the desk-bound corruption of their superiors and the pariah status that Lucas had brought upon Guatemala in the international arena. Embittered military men muttered despondently that defeat by the Left, political as well as military, was only a matter of time. When pressed for an estimate, most would guess two to three years. Droves of Guatemalan capitalists, their suitcases stuffed with U.S. dollars, began to make the trek to Miami in the wake of their Salvadorean and Nicaraguan counterparts.

That was in 1981, and in the first months of 1982. Six years, in other words, after the closing pages of *Days of the Jungle*. Over entire stretches of the highlands, with the solid backing of a sophisticated civilian support infrastructure, the Left held sway. By the time of the March 1982 elections, the movement was in a position to declare its unity—the culminating statement of a twenty-eight-year-long process of maturation, and a calculated political gauntlet thrown down to the regime at its moment of deepest crisis.

Events since then merit a separate book in themselves. History is still being written. A born-again evangelical fanatic in the National Palace is manna to those who would reduce the complex ongoing struggle to colorful anecdote and hasty political judgment. If a war can be declared speedily over and done with, no matter how distasteful the methods, then moral consciences can again quiet themselves. How was it that one network news report put it? That the Guatemalan army may be brutal, but at least it is successful—and who in the United States can argue with success?

Since General Efraín Ríos Montt seized power in the March 1982 coup, everything has changed, and nothing has changed. By Christmas time, the pipe-dream of Ríos Montt's public relations office—that the "Victoria 82" counterinsurgency masterplan had been a complete success—was being dutifully relayed over the wires to world public opinion. The war, we were told, was over.

The only rational conclusion possible after a sober study of the facts is precisely the opposite. And the signs are that the army is emerging from its scorched-earth euphoria to recognize that it has solved nothing. The objective basis of revolt—the material misery of the vast majority of Guatemalans—remains untouched. The spiralling economic crisis bites ever deeper. And the Left has survived one of the most coherent, sustained, and sanguinary counterinsurgency campaigns ever unleashed in Latin America. The massacre of anywhere between 5,000 and 10,000 unarmed Indian *campesinos,* and the uprooting of a million more from their homes, have turned the population bitterly against an army more clearly identified as the enemy than ever before. In the search for a rapid and brutal victory, the military has exhausted many of its scarce strategic reserves. The armed forces are stretched to the limit simply to preserve the fragile status quo. For the first time in twenty years, they resorted to the crude device of a *coup d'état* in order to secure their rule. In doing so, they relinquished their last shreds of legitimacy, exposing gaping rifts within the military establishment and between the army and the civilian bourgeoisie. Under Ríos Montt the whole of Guatemala is militarized, the sagging national economy further crippled by the war effort. Divide and rule is the watchword, community savagely pitted against community in the name of evangelical love. Such is Ríos Montt's Promised Land.

For the Left, the moment of triumphalism which followed the Sandinista victory in Nicaragua has passed; so has the trauma of 1982, for which even the most highly organized communities were unprepared. In the place of these extremes, the long, sober view of history has reasserted itself. This murderous war has lasted three decades already. It is not over. In terms of our public perception, and in terms of direct U.S. involvement, it has scarcely begun.

Days of the Jungle

FOREWORD

The creation of the first guerrilla detachment in the Guatemalan jungle was one of the richest and most rewarding revolutionary experiences for our organization. For those of us who cut our way through jungle vegetation with machetes, they were years of shaping and living out the political decisions we believed to be essential to revolutionary change in Guatemala. Unfortunately, the few anecdotes included here can only begin to give a sense of the wealth of meaning these early experiences had for us.

The revolutionary who does not know the inner story of those first years, and the reader who picks up these fragments for the first time, will have many questions about antecedents, objectives, achievements, and perspectives. There are understandable—and in a sense necessary—gaps. As a narrative, this is an attempt to reflect the impressions and experiences of the author, the failures and successes as he perceived them. Thus while these tales are historical testimony, they are not balanced; while they do not disregard the most important facts and situations, they do not add up to a total picture. That is a task that can only be carried out collectively, and must be left for the future. In the meantime, it was important to set down something of what we had lived through: time moves on and memories seem to be made for forgetting.

The history here described episodically is far from concluded. We still have a long road to cover. In the meantime, it

is enough to say that many of the ideas with which we originally
set out to transform the world of the northwestern Guatemalan
jungle were corrected in practice and enriched by experience.
The next few years will tell if these changes were correct. The
task is immense and our experience is limited—limited by the
environment where our guerrillas march with their burdens of
sorrow and joy. But to the extent that we build on the experiences of those who come before us, they can serve as a point of
reference for our *compañeros* on other battlefronts, perhaps even
for those in other countries who are rising up in arms under
similar conditions.

—MARIO PAYERAS

1979

JANUARY 19

On January 19, 1972, the Edgar Ibarra guerrilla detachment penetrated Guatemalan territory. This was the core of what was to become, some years later, the Guerrilla Army of the Poor. Thus ended a period of feverish preparation outside of Guatemala, which had one pressing goal: to return to Guatemala and to re-initiate the guerrilla struggle in the mountains.

The border crossing did not, however, turn out as we had planned. Our unit of twenty-five had meant to enter the country secretly and to launch the armed struggle only when we could count on a necessary base of support in the interior. The defeat we had suffered in the previous decade had been a learning experience, and one of its main lessons was the risk of improvised action. This time, therefore, we intended to do things right.

Months earlier, as part of our plan, a small group of *compañeros* had managed to settle on the banks of the Río Ixcán, passing themselves off as Mexicans. They made a clearing in a pocket of the jungle close to Guatemalan territory, and built huts on both sides of the river. While they cleared the land and planted corn, they became friendly with the people living along the river's edge. This first undertaking cost the life of one of our most valiant *compañeros*, Concepción García. He was not a good swimmer, and during one of many river crossings he was dragged away by the current. We never recovered his body. But that small jungle clearing and the palm huts he had helped build formed the secret base used during the winter of 1971 by the rest of us in our approach to the border.

Following the solitary routes used by the chicle workers and

21

settlers, a second group joined the vanguard from the Patará region, secretly crossing the few inhabited areas and traveling mostly at night. This contingent carried most of the arms and ammunition that made up our modest arsenal.

The final group arrived in December. It consisted of myself and two others, and we arrived by air, aboard a small commercial plane that made regular flights between the city of Comitán in Chiapas and the Mexican side of the Ixcán. From the air we could see vast jungle stretching as far as the horizon. On landing at the tiny airfield, we set foot in a steamy jungle world, dominated by the shrilling of cicadas and the thunder of the river waters. The heat was suffocating and we had trouble moving in the heavy atmosphere. The chicle workers, pale from the humidity and malaria, sensed that we were men of arms. That same night, the Mexican employees at the supply station told us about a bullet-ridden body that the river had dragged across from the Guatemalan side.

The first days after our arrival were peaceful. Our plan was to explore the area, to set up advance posts and to build a minimal social base that would support our war effort, using the huts on the border as our rear guard.

During the last days of the year and the first days of January we were very busy. While the group at the huts kept up appearances, the rest of us dug in our arms caches, moved equipment, and set up the first camp farther inside Guatemalan territory. We were an ant column, working from dawn to dusk. Then we hung up our hammocks, built fires, and, after a light supper of slices of tamales and spoonfuls of beans sent from the huts, listened to the evening news and bedded down.

This was a time when the most exciting event was the discovery of a jaguar's tracks. The splendid library we had built up over the months were ruined by the climate. The books containing the social knowledge of the nineteenth century were eaten by white ants and stained by the dampness. *Year One of the Russian Revolution, One Hundred Years of Solitude,* and *The Country of the Long Shadows* were all we could save. The rest we had to abandon to the rain.

The law of least effort began to govern our movements, and an order of priorities based on absolute realism ruled our lives when it came to material goods.

At about this time, an advance patrol penetrated deep into the jungle and returned with wild boar meat and hopeful news. From a treetop several days' journey ahead they had glimpsed the unmistakable blue mountains of Huehuetenango in the distance.

We spent those first days learning the basic truths of the jungle. We found ourselves in a new world, and only time would teach us its points of reference. Without these, the compass was useless. We quickly learned that it was best to ignore the plague of mosquitoes and gnats. The melancholy song of the partridge marked the hours of those early days of rain and solitude. We learned to distinguish the right leaves for wrapping tamales and the kind of reed that makes good tea and also serves for tying house posts. Those who knew the jungle taught the rest of us to differentiate between the various species of snakes. They explained the habits of the deadly coral snake, with its band of red and black rings, and described the velvety appearance of the lethal *barbamarilla*. We discovered that the *colmovote,* the worm that a mosquito buries under the skin, dies if it is soaked with the sap of the *cojón* plant or covered with a patch of ordinary adhesive tape. Although we found tapir tracks every day, it was months before some of us saw one. Meanwhile, we learned the basics of finding our bearings by observing the light and the lay of the land. For the time being we didn't venture far into that silence of moths and fireflies.

Things began to happen in the second week of January. Hunters began turning up at our huts, asking too many questions and subjecting us to veritable interrogations. We were still in a precarious situation, without a single contact in Guatemalan territory. We always kept in mind Che's defeat in Bolivia—that lone guerrilla unit in the jungle, without a peasant base of support and in constant flight—and we slept with one eye open, mistrustful of strangers and people who simply turned up.

Two years before, a few miles away on the shores of the Río Lacantún, Marco Antonio Yon Sosa and Socorro Sical, legendary guerrilla leaders, remnants of a previous period of struggle, had been murdered. Constantly pursued, exhausted by the long jungle crossing, they had hidden in Mexican territory, accompanied by two or three of their group. Yon Sosa made the mistake of believing that the Mexican officials under whose protection he placed himself had the same sense of military honor as he.

This bitter experience weighed heavily in our decision to draw up an alternative plan of action. During one long night, assailed by doubts as to the risks and advantages involved, we worked out a plan to move out of the area. We knew we would have to do it in such a way that our *compañeros* in Mexico City would be alerted. They made up another segment of our guerrilla force, and were preparing to enter the country via other routes—since at that point we could count on only one small group in Guatemala City. Tavo left to carry the news of the change of plan.

Secondly, and no less important, the plan would have to mislead the enemy as to the precariousness of our situation. At no time did we forget that once we abandoned our border base we would have to trust to luck. Under these circumstances, it made the most sense to take the initiative. Finally, from this foray we needed to obtain enough provisions for a long trek, one that we expected would take months.

The morning following January 19, in a lightning action we took the landing field, the supply station, set fire to two small planes whose owners had been involved in the murder of Yon Sosa, and disarmed and solemnly warned the suspected enemy agents to remain silent. Then, after buying a good supply of provisions, we commandeered motor boats for the trip down the Río Lacantún.

The next day found us several miles to the east, on the banks of the Río Xaclbal, hastily unloading the arms and provisions captured the day before. Once the euphoria of the action and of the hazardous trip downriver had ended, the morning light brought our tiny improvised army face to face with its real situation. Exhausted by the tension and the vigil, and haphazardly armed, we faced an enormous mountain of supplies that seemed to have emerged from the hold of a ship, rather than from two small motor boats. Commandeered arms, ammunition, packing cases, medicines, farm tools, boots, sacks of provisions, and fifteen backpacks filled to bursting awaited us a few yards from shore. In the distance, buzzing like wasps, we could make out the enemy planes that had, very early, started to search for us. The die had been cast. Behind us a combined operation by the two armies that was to go on for months was beginning—although later we learned that the Mexican army limited itself to fruitless tracking on the banks of the broad border rivers.

To the south were the Guatemalan villages that existed only on maps and in our dreams, but that were nevertheless our North Star. Ahead of us, a sea of ceiba and *conacaste* trees extended to the horizon. That day we barely managed to advance 500 yards. Burdened by the weight of full cartridge belts and backpacks, with two or three weapons piled on top and a box of medicines or a pair of boots hanging around our necks, we moved very slowly. Our clothes were torn to shreds as we pushed our way through the dense vegetation—we avoided cutting a path so as not to leave a trail. When, balancing carefully so as not to topple over, we descended to the bed of a ravine, our boots sank deep into the mire and there we were, stuck. Only by walking in pairs were we able to reach the other side, after sliding back time and time again. Only Chacaj, an experienced carrier, was able to carry over a hundredweight on his back, one hand on his *mecapal,* or headband, breathing rhythmically and moving across obstacles without changing his pace. For those of us not used to this traditional form of carrying a load suspended from a headband, the *mecapal* was a nuisance: it would slip down, cutting off our vision. Then we would decide to carry the weight on our shoulders, although this meant sores and unbearable pain. Or we would try the *tahali,* a primitive harness, or the strap of a weapon, or one of our many horse harnesses, although these slowed us down when they caught on a branch or trunk. If anyone, at those moments, had talked to us about taking power and building a socialist society, we would probably have told him to drop dead. When we finally reached firm ground, drenched with sweat, Chacaj would have already set down his load and be returning from his second trip to the river bank. That night we flopped down, utterly spent, ten minutes from the beach, after a long battle to make a fire with wet wood.

It was under these conditions that we embarked upon our

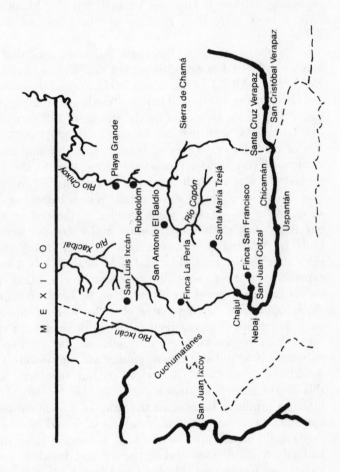

District of Ixcán in Northeast Guatemala

MEXICO

Río Chixoy

Río Xacbal

Río Ixcán

San Juan Ixcoy

Cuchumatanes

Playa Grande

Rubelolóm

San Luis Ixcán

San Antonio El Baldío

Finca La Perla

Chajul

Nebaj

San Juan Cotzal

Finca San Francisco

Santa María Tzejá

Río Copón

Sierra de Chamá

Chicamán

Uspantán

Santa Cruz Verapaz

San Cristóbal Verapaz

crossing of the jungle. The army helicopters began whirring at dawn and stopped only at night, constantly on the lookout for our smoke or light. Although in fact the choppers' success was nil, they did pass right over our camp on several occasions. After the first time this happened, marching groups were organized, sentry schedules set up, and rules for silence fixed.

The difficult days of the initial stage began. We found, after an inventory of food and equipment, that the latter made up most of our load. With discipline and rational planning, we had enough oil, rice, salt, and sugar for twenty days. Further on we would pick up the small amount of corn that we had been able to store in our strategic supply depots. These might last for a month, but we did not know how long our march would be.

"Discipline and rational planning" meant that, since the entire day's ration supplied enough energy for only one or two hours of marching—and we marched from dawn to dusk—the rest of our energy had to come from the more abundant cupboards of our revolutionary morale and willpower. After one week on such a diet, our occasional chats during rest periods, our conversation after mess, and many of our dreams were about food. And food was the most important subject of our long nightly meetings.

In an unmistakable tone of reprimand, Sebastián would begin: "Today at breakfast there was an incident..." We all knew what would follow. It always had to do with the "abundant cupboard." The guilty comrade would speak and, rambling on for an hour or more and giving explanations that Sebastián had summarized in five minutes, would end by acknowledging that he had in fact licked the empty sugar sack when he should have soaked it in the water used for making coffee, thus economizing on the sugar ration. At 10 o'clock, nodding sleepily, we would listen to the final summing up of the evening's session and go to our hammocks, each of us solemnly promising himself that he would never be guilty of a crime against the collective economy. This was our initiation, and our survival was definitely made possible by its lessons.

At about this time we made another of our three great "discoveries"—corn flour. (The first, of course, had been plastic. Without it one simply cannot survive in a world where it rains

nine months out of the year. The discovery of the third item—
rubber boots—still lay far in the future, after months of constant marching with wet feet.) Our discovery consisted of the
following: with a hand grinder, easily obtained from the peasants, we could grind the dried corn to a fine flour. This saved
us precious time because it cooked quickly, and it saved space
because it reduced the volume of corn. But although this system
undoubtedly meant an important saving of time and corn, it
also led to increased malnutrition. Later we found that by syste-
matic hunting we could increase our protein intake, but in the
beginning there were few opportunities to hunt, and few among
us were experienced hunters. However, the game we did bag
we devoured almost whole. Except for the feathers, claws, and
some of the cartilage, the entire animal was cooked and shared
equally—including the bones. These, grilled on the coals, were
first-class food in times of hunger.

During the second week's march something extraordinary
happened. One day, soon after crossing the Río Piedras Blancas,
our scouts found a bundle wrapped in plastic and hanging from
a tree. After careful reconnoitering, we cautiously explored the
area. There was a trail running north to south that had been cut
not more than three months before. The swaths ended below
the branches of the tree where the mysterious bundle hung. Sus-
pecting a trap, we retreated for a while and watched. After
perhaps an hour, and with extreme care, we approached the
bundle. It was carefully tied and smelled unmistakably of food.
In fact, it contained provisions left there for some unknown
reason. There were salt, hardboiled eggs, powdered dried chili,
and dried tortillas, enough for several days. Maybe it belonged
to those who had cut the path and were temporarily away—
but it could have also been a trap set by the enemy.

One member of the patrol, goaded by his rumbling belly,
did not discount the possibility of the food's having been left for
us by sympathetic peasants. He proposed that we accept the gift
and consume it on the spot. However, we left without touching
the food and returned to tell the rest of the unit about our
find. The next day, after discussing the matter, we went back
and carried it off. We left a message wrapped in a bit of plastic
and hanging from the cord, explaining who we were and the

reasons for our struggle, along with money to cover the cost of what we took. Months later we learned that the supplies had belonged to some trackers who had found our message and the money. That small incident became our best letter of introduction, since the story of our honesty went from person to person and in time spread throughout the entire area.

We continued east for several days, always following makeshift maps. Since helicopters were constantly flying over us, we moved with the utmost caution. Aside from their persistent noise, the only sounds that broke the silence were the sudden stampede of wild boar and the distant squawk of parrots. Sometimes we found fallen ceiba trees whose tremendous trunks were far longer than our column.

We no longer saw sunlight and began to lose our sense of time. Surely we were the first humans in centuries to pass through that jungle. From time to time, when digging latrine holes, we turned up Indian artifacts. They bore witness to the fact that the routes followed by the great human migrations of the past had crossed this area.

We rose at dawn, awakened by screeching birds, and marched all day in near silence. We had more than enough time to think over our commitment, to scrutinize our deepest class-based motivations. What did each of us think about during those interminable days?

We were a mosaic of ethnic and social backgrounds. Lacho, Jorge, Julián, and Mario were Achí and Cakchikel Indians, yet despite their common language and culture they did not form a homogeneous group. Lacho was preoccupied by the enigmas and sufferings of his Indian identity in the midst of a culture at once alien and attractive to him. The others did not agonize so much over these problems, but were more concerned with the basic fact that people organize and divide the world impelled by material interests.

Chacaj, Toribio, Atilio, Jacobo, and Efraín were from the Pacific Coast and all had been exploited to some degree. All had occupied different positions in the mercantile economy of that region, and thus had been led to think in different ways. Questions of property ownership and manual labor, their reading, childhood poverty and misery common to all of them under the law of capitalism both separated and united them, but had ultimately led them to rebel.

Alejandro and Minche were from the eastern region. Although both were of peasant stock, their circumstances differed. Alejandro was very poor and Minche relatively well off. They sprouted from the same earth, but each had developed differently. Alejandro was a flowering orange tree, Minche a prickly cactus.

Sebastián, Víctor, Edgar, and Benedicto came from cities and had acquired a certain amount of learning as well as certain weaknesses. They had learned dialectics—that matter is in constant motion—but their weakness prevented them from changing their mental attitude with a speed equal to that of the atoms they knew moved within all things.

All fifteen of us marched together. Only time would mature each enough to bear his fruit. Our leadership was collective, and our leaders were veterans of Las Minas mountain and of the earlier urban resistance. One of them, Víctor, persisted in orienting himself in the jungle with a compass and maps of the past decade, to which the guerrillas were never to return. He knew how to lead our small force militarily, but the idea of the guerrilla unit as a seed that must be at once an army and a political organization was never part of his perspective. He never understood that we were not there simply to vindicate his name, but rather to create a new kind of truth. We were beginning to realize that many experiences lay ahead of us, and we already knew that history is made by groups, not by individuals.

Our next discovery was that in the jungle time is measured by sounds. When the sun rises and the din of the first hours has ended, only the call of the wild pigeon lingers on in the late morning. In some areas the roar of the monkeys, or the clarion call of turkey hens in flight, marked the horizon. When we heard this we knew it was time for the midday meal, and we ate what we had saved from breakfast. At dusk the screeching of the parrots and macaws signaled the hour for carrying wood, building a fire, and hanging our hammocks. Then began the hours when the birds were silent and we heard only the night mammals. The damp tropical night was filled with the screaming of the coatis and the self-criticism of our group sessions. Near the river time was measured until dawn by the intermittent song of tropical birds.

An identical routine was followed each day. As we marched, we would pass large trees filled with chattering monkeys. After several weeks of living by the zoological clock, the jungle seemed to us to be an endless ocean that we sailed with no definite itinerary, toward no specific port. Behind us lay only the fluttering of the huge jungle butterflies.

One month after our border action we reached the swamps further up the Río Xaclbal. This was a memorable moment in the history of our guerrilla detachment, for there we found the first signs of habitation. We came upon a Seville orange tree growing in the shade of the forest, blossoming according to an altered calendar due to the lack of sunlight: although it was February, it still retained its meager fruits of the previous year.

There, Toribio killed two deer. Their meat and that of several wild turkeys relieved our gnawing hunger.

After crossing half a jungle, we were a hungry and ragged army. The paleness peculiar to those who have lived for a long time without sunlight and the stench of our sweaty clothes identified our column of shadow-men as we advanced, guided mostly by instinct. Most of us were bone-thin and carried out each day's march as a way of forgetting our obsessive hunger. Our stock of corn was almost finished, and we had sugar enough for one or two days at most. Our oil had given out the previous week. The day before we had hacked down virtually a whole forest searching for honeycombs, but unfortunately this raw food caused severe stomach cramps and constant diarrhea. If we had not reached that first village at just that moment, our situation would have become extremely difficult.

Nevertheless, our proximity to inhabited areas also meant the risk of running into the enemy. The dead calm of the jungle we had traveled through could only mean that the government soldiers were waiting for us in more populated spots. Our sense of hope and danger was thus mixed with apprehension about the villagers' response to us. Alejandro, when he reflected on what a tiny group we were, sometimes predicted that there would soon be a long column of recruits marching with us. This demonstrated his limitless faith in the people. But more often he talked about the terror he had witnessed in the villages near Zacapa during the army's anti-guerrilla attacks in 1966 and 1967. He had seen huts burned down and peasants who had collaborated with the guerrillas suddenly fleeing from them. Thus, as we came upon more and more signs of habitation we all experienced a growing tension. At the same time, we realized that we were living the most beautiful adventure of our lives.

The day we finished the last of our corn, we came across a trail that must have been cut some two years earlier. The day before we had forded the Río Xaclbal and we were walking south, looking for a village that was only a dot on the map. That morning we followed the trail to the southeast, moving closer to the river. By afternoon we found a weed-infested garden near the bank. The sudden shrieks of magpies kept us on the alert. From there on the footpath was perfectly visible and continued south. But darkness obliged us to stop, and we hung our hammocks close to an old trackers' camp in a stand of palm trees.

Before going to sleep we devoured the remaining ration of venison and a bit of rice saved for the last moment. At dawn we renewed our march, but redoubled our precautions since it was obvious that we were approaching a hamlet. In the mud, preserved by the humid shade of the jungle, we found the first tracks of shod feet, although they were very old tracks. On top of these we could make out the onion-shaped marks of a dog's paws. At noon the scout patrol reported that they had found a deserted hut in a small clearing where a chili bush grew. The forked poles that supported the thatched roof were white with bird droppings, and in the surrounding area we found only the tracks of wild animals. The worn old trail continued south, snaking across old forest growth that snapped with a sharp echo whenever we broke a branch.

In the early afternoon we got word that our scouts had come upon some huts. We were ordered to hide alongside the path, which appeared to be frequently used. All we could see of the village was the bright light of the cleared area and here and there old axe marks on tree trunks. In the jungle there was deep silence, only faintly broken by the gentle movement of the birds in the topmost branches.

For a long time we waited, listening to our hearts beat. Then a rooster crowed in the direction of the village. It was the first time in months that we had heard that pleasing call. We exchanged looks that were a mixture of anxiety and joy. There they were at last, our country's poor, but we had no idea how they would respond to us. As time passed we identified other sounds—the clucking of hens, distant machete chops, the voices of women calling their chickens. Suddenly the sharp barking of dogs. For us, waiting with our hearts in our mouths, this was an unmistakable sign that our *compañeros* had approached the villagers. We knew that at that moment, for better or for worse, our fate was being decided.

The next few minutes were extremely tense, but we knew by our *compañero*'s manner of walking and expression that he brought good news. In fact, it couldn't have been better. In his explorations around the hamlet he had found only old tracks and no sign of the enemy. As the scouts neared the houses, our *compañero* reported, a thin bushy-browed boy with a deep voice had greeted them familiarly, showing no surprise at their weapons or outfits, and had told them that just the day before the villagers had been talking about us.

There were six families in all, recently settled in that small clearing. They had heard over the radio about our action at the border. They had no corn, but they were willing to share whatever else they had. That night we met with the men of the village. We explained the purpose of our struggle, and solemnly announced that we would triumph.

RUBELOLOM

Our days in the village taught us much about the conditions of our people and the difficulties inherent in their struggle for freedom. The villagers had come from all the regions of the country, having settled in the jungle after suffering indescribable misfortunes. Most of them were illiterate and their only link to the outside world was the radio. Except for their access to sunlight and their sedentary life, their day-to-day conditions were in many ways not unlike ours in the worst of times. Instead of walking for hours every day, they had to chop down centuries-old trees with only the strength of their arms and the aid of an axe. They had come looking for land at a time when there were not even any roads into the jungle. This was the northernmost inhabited area of Ixcán. We had come upon it by chance, since the place we had actually been looking for existed only on the map. The settlers didn't even know that a market had been set up months earlier on the other side of the river. They survived on corn bought several miles away, supplemented by wild plants or by game that they hunted when they had ammunition. Their ailments were typical of malnutrition. They asked us for medicine to cure illnesses that only a total change of the social order could remedy.

The next day we got to work. We split up into teams to help them with their work in the fields, which required many hands. We treated small infections, repaired broken-down doors, chopped wood. This was the best way of explaining to them what the poor of Guatemala must do. When we left—with our backpacks just as empty as when we arrived—we at least had the satisfaction of having planted the seeds of a friendship that time would not destroy.

But our own situation had not substantially improved. There would be no corn in the area until August. We were beginning to understand the lesson of the first period: to adjust our routine to the passing of the seasons.

In the hamlet we had been told that a few hours away there was a larger village where a market was held on certain days. We set out to find it. We were convinced that only by establishing roots among the people could we survive in the long run, and that only by stationing ourselves in densely populated areas tied into the market economy could we really expand the armed struggle.

One morning, from a small rise, we looked out over the panorama of the jungle. It was the month of the *tamborillo* tree, and its yellow blossoms spread unforgettably before us. To the south, awesomely close to the sky, were the great peaks of the northern Chamá range, an objective still beyond our reach. There, several miles to the north, we were sure there were

Indian settlements where guerrilla armies would be organized in the foreseeable future. We allowed ourselves to dream a while, but our reality was the jungle with its dangers, its loneliness, and its huge distances.

We got lost on the desolate trails in our search for the village of Santa María Tzejá, but because of the height, for the first time we didn't sweat as we marched. That night we slept on the banks of the Río Tzejá, having completely lost our bearings. The next day we continued along the edge of El Cantil, a small rocky range of hills with great caves full of bats where the Indians of the region lit candles to their secret gods and celebrated ancient rites. Several miles to the east we finally came across an Indian town, part of the municipality of Uspantán. On learning of our presence, the inhabitants either locked themselves into their houses or fled to the hills. Suddenly the situation became dramatic. Some of us were forced to chase after the runaways and warn them to return. Those were moments we'll never forget. Suddenly we found ourselves walking deserted streets. The few remaining inhabitants who might have talked to us barricaded themselves behind their dialect and it was impossible to get any information from them, or even to purchase food.

The place was called Dolores. Two dry tortillas for each of us and vague references to the town we were looking for were all we could get from its inhabitants. There, for the first time, we heard the word *macá*—a terrible word which for us at the time meant something far worse than "there isn't any" because it was a rejection that had its roots in the past. We could see, in the granaries of the very people who told us that they had no corn, mounds of what we needed so badly in order to survive.

On the road once again, we came across traders from distant towns. Greeting us with low, guttural sounds, reserved and at the same time threatening, they answered our questions evasively. Of course, they could not know that many years down the road our paths would cross again.

Later we understood some of the reasons for their mistrust. Years before, an armed patrol of guerrillas had passed through and camped for some days in the village on their way south. In full view of all the villagers, they had killed a pig sold to them by a community leader, eaten it, and continued on their way. The reaction of the government soldiers who came to the town later, searching for the guerrillas, was not surprising. Under orders of a particularly harsh officer, the troops captured the man who had sold the pig, tied him up, and kept his body floating in the river for a week. They strung up many other villagers from trees, and held several mock executions.

After a brief look around Santa María Tzejá, we returned to the jungle, having spent almost all our money in the village stores. In order to mislead possible informers, we had, on our arrival, pretended to be an antiguerrilla patrol and had also pretended to force the traders into selling to us, although such was not the case. But thanks to such strategems, the enemy could do little more than note our presence in the area.

We returned via the Río Tzejá on a kayak loaded with our purchases. This was the most hazardous of our treks, because we became separated by the twists and turns of the river, and had to make our way through an area completely unfamiliar to us. Our kayak overturned in the swift current, and we lost our way again and again. We walked along muddy roads in complete darkness because our flashlight batteries had gone dead several weeks before. Finally, by some miracle, we all met up again, and spent the night drying out around the fire. The next morning we heard on the radio the distant voice of a colonel asking if there were signs that we were in the area.

For a few days our constant hunger was assuaged by the food we had bought, although as always we got diarrhea from the change in diet. Our digestive systems underwent extreme shifts. A few days before some of us had been so constipated that we had had to use our fingers to help evacuate our bowels, because the lack of fats and the constant dehydration due to the heat had dried out our intestines. Our defecations were hard and rough and caused painful bleeding. During the sieges of diarrhea, however, it was as though there were a direct passageway from our mouths to our anuses. We would not quite finish a glass of liquid before we had to run to the bush, bathed in cold sweat, our guts bursting—or, lamentably, already loosened.

For one glorious week we were able to smoke again, since

our purchases included this vital war supply. Despite the pleasure and comfort it provided, tobacco was always a source of discord among us. The habitual smoker was either slandered or otherwise mistreated. The *guerrillero* who had had the foresight to preserve a cigarette butt through storms and overturned boats, and who set out to enjoy it in his hammock after a grueling day, was inevitably reprimanded by a *compañero* with less foresight for "acting like a thief, giving free rein to his individualism."

It was always a problem. But our constant search for tobacco also taught us a lesson in revolutionary patience. One day when we were in a hamlet, one of us who for weeks had had to make do with smoking *guarumo* leaves, thinking that our return to civilization meant the end of his long deprivation, had asked the owner of one of the huts if he had any tobacco. He was filled with joy when he was told yes. Our *compañero* who had shown such initiative cast a triumphant glance at the rest of us smokers. Each of us was imagining a thick cluster of smooth pale leaves. Our gracious host led us to his patio and showed us a tiny tobacco plant in a clay pot. With the aid of the March sunshine, the plant would surely have flourished, in due course, giving its owner—who measured time by the seasons—much satisfaction. This was a lesson in the importance of patience, especially for us, planters of the slow-growing tree of revolution.

Our rations of corn, salt, and sugar permitted us to begin moving toward the Río Chixoy, the natural boundary between Ixcán and the Alta Verapaz regions. We were obsessed with the desire to reach populated areas and the Verapaz zones drew us like a magnet. In spite of being deprived and pursued, we felt strong enough to take on any venture that would end our isolation.

By then we were becoming used to the rigors of life in the jungle. Some of us had even become good hunters. On days of forced inactivity they would go out early in the morning to learn the birds' flight paths. Once they had detected their feeding spots, we were assured of game as long as we had bullets. They would return to camp in the evening loaded down with pheasant and wild turkey. The bagging of a wild boar was a chance occurrence, since these animals don't follow fixed routes. Their peculiar odor, or the snapping of their jaws, is their signal. After a rapid strike, which usually felled three or four boar, the entire unit would bring them back to camp and butcher them. Competing with great swarms of green flies that in no time covered the meat, we would cut it up into long strips which we roasted slowly over the fire. We would dry some for future consumption—thus we often had reserves enough for several weeks.

At this point our life was regulated by periods of hunger and marching. We rose with the first light and cooked breakfast while listening to the 6 o'clock news. When it ended at 7 we doled out our flour ration. Each of us was free to eat his entire portion or save some of it for noon, since the fires would not be lit again until dark. Those with enough willpower would set aside about one-third of their portion in a small sardine tin. The thought of that cold, insipid mush would obsess us all morning long. The most self-controlled could last until 10 o'clock with his ration intact. Some persisted in this test of willpower; most gave up after two or three failures.

By 8 o'clock we were ready to move on. That was also the time when we listened to the international news—the Voice of America was the only program that could travel through the humid ether to our radio. Thus the difficult task of getting underway coincided with the tinkly Broadway tune that was the program's theme song. Even today when we hear that melody we immediately recall our days of eating raw bamboo shoots and the rest stops on the march when we napped, waiting for our scouts to cut a swath through the jungle, pursued by swarms of bees that collected the salt from our first morning sweat.

One memorable event on the march toward the Chixoy was the deer hunt. Víctor and Julián were the protagonists of this adventure. Víctor, out on a routine hunt, was following the river when he saw the animal. He lost sight of it for a while, but then was surprised by the sound of the galloping hooves of a fat buck. He kept his rifle cocked and several shots found their target. The gravely wounded animal jumped into the river and managed to reach the opposite shore. But Julián, having been attracted by the shots and the noise, was there waiting for him.

Machete in hand, he threw himself onto the frightened animal and finished him off. The two hunters transported the enormous carcass on the river's current to our camp. When we pulled it ashore, its tender tongue protruding, we became aware of its great weight. Its flanks were covered with ticks, and it was already rigid in death. Its dried meat fed us for many days.

It was already March when we reached the banks of the Chixoy. At last we were approaching the outer edge of the uninhabited world that had for several months been the scene of our long march. We began hearing the Kekchí dialect and discovering the taciturnity of the people. At the same time, all kinds of pleasing news was reaching us. We learned that the river was a regular commercial route and that there were small sugar mills in some of the river villages. Most of the inhabitants were squatters who had settled there long before. They owned considerable land, won from the endless jungle with the machete.

Flights of macaws across the open sky and the intense light reminded us once again of the real dimensions of space after months of living in the murky shadows cast by the huge trees and our rush candles. The villagers watched us with a mixture of astonishment and pity, taking in the rags, skeletal thinness, shaggy beards and hair, and hungry stares of a group of castaways spewed out by the jungle.

A bigamous and racist *ladino,* willing to help us out of self-interest, sold us some hens and a bunch of cigars, while he bustled about his house, extremely nervous, clapping his hands to urge on his Indian wives who were busily patting out tortillas for our lunch. He told us that up river there was a village where we could probably buy supplies.

The next day we followed the solitary river path and came upon some dwellings. It was a dispersed village in the shade of giant trees on the banks of the river. No one seemed to be about, as the houses were shut and silence answered our call. There were broken down bird cages in some of the patios. Flowers grew around the support posts of the houses, blossoming inside.

In a communal hut we found our first living being: an old Indian man, lying on a cot, his head bound in a kerchief, wracked with fever. He sat up with difficulty. He had the brilliant gaze, thin face, and gasping voice of someone with advanced lung disease. He said the place was called Rubelolóm, and that its inhabitants were Kekchí Indians from Alta Verapaz who had arrived many years before looking for land and fleeing from the injustices of the local officials. He said they had no salt, or corn, or any of the things we needed.

The people in the next house were willing to sell us a bunch of bananas for a very high price. It was the same with some game two young hunters had for sale. No one would speak more than two or three words of Spanish to us, and no one understood our *compañeros* who spoke Achí. They claimed not to know where the roads led, or the location of any other villages. They still lived in an age of wooden tools, and many hunted with traps and slingshots. We wandered about the hamlet for two or three days, collecting small amounts of salt and fruit, moving with extreme caution.

We were very suspicious of the silence that prevailed and the indifference of the inhabitants. At several points we had unknowingly missed the enemy by minutes. They too were in the area, moving with equal caution but using trained dogs. On the banks of the river we often found empty tins of army rations dropped by helicopter for the ground troops.

A few days later, on March 13, the jungle's silence was shattered by the sound of shots. One of our scouts had gone to get some sweet potatoes from a field when he heard the unmistakable sound of a bullet whizzing by close to his temple. He had probably been fired at from the bushes with a silenced gun, because he heard only a muffled detonation. This was enough to alert us. The scout soon saw the first dog emerge from behind a rise. His master followed, but was distracted by something behind him. Without losing a second, our *compañero* took aim and fired. The soldier fell on his back, shouting something. The others, surprised, opened fire and continued shooting for about half an hour. The retreating scout heard the sound of gunfire for a long time.

Meanwhile, back at camp, we were missing a member of our group who had gone hunting at dawn and not returned by noon. Our anxiety grew when, early in the afternoon, our scout reported distant, barely audible, shots. It was a difficult moment because, had an encounter with the enemy occurred, we would have had to move on, yet we could not have left one of our members behind. We immediately dispatched search parties.

In that short spell our lost comrade lived through the most anguished moments of his life. To be lost in the jungle is in itself a harrowing, although instructive, experience, but under those circumstances, armed only with a .22 caliber rifle, with no camping equipment or food, and at a time when we had neither a fixed camp nor a base of support among the people, it meant either complete withdrawal from our guerrilla force or capture.

Finding our lost *compañero* in that jungle universe was like finding a needle in a haystack. We decided that, propelled by hunger and isolation, he would sooner or later have to emerge in some inhabited place, and that there he was sure to encounter the enemy. The only way he could re-establish connections with the organization was by contacting a woman *compañera* in the city or through an old address in Mexico. On the other hand, he knew he was south of the trail of our march toward Chixoy, which lay more or less east. Thus by establishing north and south, he might be able to pick up our trail. But with no compass and no reference points, he could not locate north. To make matters worse, it was a very cloudy day, which made it impossible to find the position of the sun. The same diffuse light was everywhere. Nevertheless, he tried the method of sticking a twig in the ground and deducing the sun's path from its shadow, taking into account variations due to the time of the year. Unfortunately, the twig threw no shadow whatsoever, so dim was the light.

Next he cut several exploratory trails, trying to locate some recognizable spot without losing his way back to his starting point. Everywhere he found trails with growth dating several years back. They marked old hunters' trails and led nowhere. The bird calls were no help either, since he did not know the habits of the birds in the area. As the hours passed and his efforts failed, he became confused. This is something anyone who is lost must avoid at all costs. Finding one's way depends on maintaining one's common sense and remaining calm. Having lost both, he decided to follow his instinct as to where north lay, combining his questionable suppositions about the light, humidity and so on. As he advanced, trying not to stray from the imagined route, he began walking faster. Earlier that morning he had caught a squirrel, but in his desperate determination to move on he had tossed it away, and in any case his lighter had failed, so it was pointless to think of starting a fire for cooking.

Almost at a run, he crossed swampy areas and totally unrecognizable ravines where he found only old wild boar tracks. At dusk he saw a giant boa slithering toward some unknown destination, and felt even more disconsolate. It was almost dark when he found the first trace of the guerrilla group. He had come upon one of our last campsites. From there it was easy to reconstruct the route taken by the column the preceding week to the site he had left the day before. Those who reach camp after having been lost arrive with a peculiar light in their eyes that is difficult to forget.

DAYS, NIGHTS, AND WEAPONS

Our experience in Rubelolóm should have taught us that the problem of survival required more complex solutions than we had imagined, and that we could not simply station ourselves in populated areas. However, for awhile we completely lost our perspective. We even discussed issuing our first war bulletin— at a time when we had no communication with the outside world. The urge to engage in combat was a kind of mirage on our horizon. In our desperation we almost believed that the indifference of the people was the result of fear and a lack of confidence in our military project. This explanation was by no means illogical. To believe in the possible victory of an army in tatters was almost impossible for men who had grown accustomed to trusting in concrete realities.

But reality itself dissuaded us from deciding on battle as an immediate possibility. We could not shoot our way to the truth when the protagonists themselves did not even understand the phenomenon of gunpowder. The use of firearms would have to await a more opportune moment. Much would have to happen before the inhabitants of that world would be willing to make our cause their own. It was not with words or with inexplicable armed encounters that we would convince them of the justice of our program. In order that our great plans might begin to take shape, our small nomadic troop would have to change its habits and, in a more settled existence, discover life's truths.

After leaving Rubelolóm we went back to our earlier stopping places. We sought out the only village where luck had smiled on us and where we were sure that perseverance would bear fruit. It was a correct decision, because we then had the good fortune of getting to know some extraordinary human beings.

Many days later, back in that area, after hours of keeping watch on the houses and observing the villagers coming and going, we once again saw the first Guatemalans we had met in February. They had not forgotten us. In our absence they had built a raft, crossed the river, and gone into the jungle looking for the supplies essential to a guerrilla troop's survival.

To our forest clearing, unbeknownst even to their families, they brought us a marvelous assortment of goods: salt, sugarloaves, bread, fish hooks, plastic, in cases carefully wrapped to preserve the goods from the humidity and even from their own temptation. From then on it was clear who among these men was going to grow upright and who would bend.

A reserved and honest giant of a man with a Biblical name, who from his youth had learned the essentials of life in the jungle—and who took pride in the wisdom he had acquired in his long life—gave us the gift of his heartfelt encouragement and solidarity, in words that still resound in our memories. Another solemn man, of few words but great strength of character, conveyed to us with a glance that he understood us and that we could count on him. A third was the long-legged, beetle-browed lad we had met before. Each took on a pseudonym, and from then on one of us stayed with them to keep watch over that first flame of devotion.

We never knew if our happiness during that period was due to our sudden change of luck or to the advent of spring. The forest smelled of honey and our path was carpeted with yellow flowers. But during the two months of our long march back to the border huts to pick up the grain and other supplies abandoned in our initial trek—which we would need while waiting for the harvest in our new home—someone would begin to sing "Atotonilco," and its music and words expressed our state of mind beautifully. Soon the others would ask Sebastián, who knew the words, to sing, as they whistled along:

> Move on, little train, to Atotonilco
> Move on, my love awaits me there
> We're almost at the station
> And my heart leaps for joy . . .

We found one cornfield intact in the hamlet, and buried underground were axes, pots, and other implements of incalculable value to us. The metal utensils were the only ones that had resisted the relentless effects of the rain. Canvas, leather, and stored foodstuffs were ruined. Although the metal parts of the rifles were intact, the wooden sections were riddled with the curious tunnels that termites chew in a matter of hours. Nevertheless, those small disasters, so frequent in our lives, had, from then on, less menacing overtones, since we felt there were better times ahead.

We then discovered that the jungle is the only place in the world where spiderwebs are not a sign of the long passage of time, but are one of the felicitous ways in which its passage can be measured. On returning along a path, we would find that a web we had torn an hour earlier had been completely respun.

Our first photos date from this time. They reflect the period of our unit's youth, when we walked along the April paths singing:

> In Atotonilco of the orange trees in blossom
> The girls are all little angels of God
> Prettier than a love song . . .

And we went along, humming when we didn't know the words:

> Atotonilco, your sky
> Has a youthful beauty
> Like a rose glowing in the midst of your silence
> Your women are lovely as rosebuds . . .
> Tatatum tatum tateee . . .

Despite our growing friendship with the villagers, our ways were still mysterious to them. They never knew where we were going or whether they would see us again. They talked about us constantly and some of them began to show a growing desire to share our dangerous life.

Once, during one of our surprise appearances, there was an incident which reflected the conditions we were experiencing. Two of the villagers were hunting and fishing downriver, a day's walk from the village. Luck was with them because the day before they had killed a tapir. They were drying the large slab of meat on the beach, accompanied by their dogs. Aware of our penury, and knowing that the two of them could not carry that much meat back to the village, they shared a good part of it with us. They also gave us the rest of the provisions they had taken along for the hunt. We distributed each portion carefully. However, at the moment of parting the villagers threw what was left of their tortillas to their dogs, probably because they were spoiled. The dogs hesitated—a fatal error—and their meal disappeared as if by magic!

From this time forward, our fortunes slowly but progressively changed for the better. One day the helicopter flights stopped completely, as suddenly as they had begun, and the jungle's silence was again unbroken except for the occasional calls of the parrots. There began interminable months of marches and countermarches that taught us how to wait and how, during the wait, to acquire more of the wisdom of the jungle.

We learned how to butcher animals and how to gather from the vegetable kingdom its rare resources: palm nuts, palm shoots, sapodilla, *zunzas*. . . . We learned how to get our bearings, how to distinguish among the forest's thousand sounds, and we began to learn the science of calculating the age of new growth, as well as of deciphering foot- and paw-prints, gauging the depth of rivers, and learning to tell direction from the stars. We re-established communication with the city and our whereabouts became known again to those outside the country who had searched for news of us in the press.

As the first harvest drew near and paths were cleared between villages, shortening distances and making our day's work more fruitful, we began to receive food supplies and had regular access to some of the manufactured goods vital to us. From our jungle refuge we patiently cultivated the friendship of the villagers, and hopefully watched the passage of time.

The season arrived for building huts in the forest and storing grain, which we did to provide for the winter and for eventual enemy offensives. One day, without our noticing it, the days of hunger had gone and the dictatorship of Atilio, the Robespierre who watched over our rations, had ceased.

This was a period of great invention and of learning sedentary ways. We invented bread, discovered rubber boots, and learned to sail a raft. Jacobo, Jorge, and some of those who had lived on the coast or in the countryside were good fishermen. They would go out late at night, and next morning there would be a string of thirty or more fish in the kitchen. Our camp began to take on a new look, and for the first time we had time to read and to examine some of our more important experiences. We built rudimentary navigation devices with balsa wood and bamboo, and transported our provisions and equipment into the jungle. We were the only inhabitants for miles around. One of us used to say that we had the largest house in the world, where water, light, and heat were free, and there was no rent.

With the rains came malaria and the scourges of the rainy season. All of June seemed to be filled with mosquitoes. When we slapped at them on our arms we left a bloody mass of insects. Smoke didn't affect them, and it was so hot that we couldn't hide under the blankets. Night did not bring the relief we hoped for—their irritating music would only rise in volume. When we lifted our spoons we would find mosquitoes in our mouths. The great downpours announced themselves with drumrolls and flashes of lightning. The rainy season also brought days of anguish and uncertainty, in which we forded rivers with the water up to our necks, carrying arms and equipment on our heads, scarcely touching bottom with the tips of our boots while we tried to slowly move with the current. At other times we crossed on rafts that were blown hither and yon by the wind. We would often reach shore several miles down river, where we would round a bend and be thrown onto a safe beach.

The rains stopped nine months later, in January. We could once again see the stars above the clearing. In February the ephemeral spring would make the *tamborillo* blossom. Then March, the month of the horse fly, of great equatorial heat and swarms of ticks. We bore all this patiently, for by then we understood that the task we had undertaken was a matter of years, and that it was right that it should be so. Those were unforgettable days, when we made the decision to dedicate not only our youth but the rest of our lives to our task.

But not all of us graduated from this extraordinary school. One of the original fifteen, Efraín, deserted during the first year. He was a good talker, a likeable fellow and very helpful, but somehow his revolutionary conviction had been undermined by unknown factors in his early life.

Whenever anyone referred to his age, he would answer: "Old is the sea, but it still provides fish." Despite his joviality and the good humor with which he seemed to accept the daily routine, he secretly resented the privations we had to undergo and remembered all too vividly the good days when he could eat yucca and dried pork. Perhaps even then he had made up his mind not to go on with us if an opportunity for leaving arose. The occasion arrived when a sore foot obliged us to let him go to the city for treatment. He was impatient with his illness and resorted to all kinds of home remedies, but to no avail. We never saw him again. We learned later that he had sought out his old bosses and returned to his old job as a store clerk.

We were, unfortunately, forced to execute Minche, another of our *compañeros*. It was a drastic, painful decision, the culmination of a process during which we exhausted our ability to save him. His problems began a few weeks after we entered Guatemala and reached the crisis point several months later. Minche was a young *compañero* from the eastern part of the country. He was robust and vigorous—after four nomadic months he was one of the few who was still healthy. He had done his military service with the government army and was always on his guard. During the years of reactionary terror in the agricultural areas, he had fled because he and his family had cooperated with the guerrillas and were in danger of execution.

At first he worked efficiently, carrying out the same tasks as the rest of us, but he stood out for his suspiciousness regarding everything related to our security. This was probably inherent in his character because we gradually came to realize that he was suspicious of any collective decision that threatened his personal interests. This reached a critical point in the matter of food. He would become excessively irritated by the involuntary injustices committed by whoever was on kitchen duty, and once he was angered there was no way to regain his trust. He bore grudges and lost no chance to get even. Furthermore, during critical moments he attempted to demoralize us, and ultimately this became a problem. When hunger was a crucial issue for all of us, he openly proclaimed his skepticism about our chances for improving our lot. He doubted our ability to win the people's support, and belittled the peasants' first modest contributions to our welfare.

We were aware of what was happening and tried our best to help him. We were particularly careful to give him a precisely equal share of the rations and tasks, and we spent many hours of our nightly meetings discussing his case. We tried to appeal to his better judgment and to win him over again for the group. However, as time passed the chasm between him and the rest of us became wider and wider. During the return to Chixoy he took to lagging far behind, which of course aroused our suspicions. It seems that he purposely created numerous petty incidents, perhaps trying to provoke our ill will and thus have a pretext for abandoning us. He did not appear to understand that, given our situation, we could not let that happen because our common security was at stake. Finally he announced that he was the victim of a general conspiracy to isolate him. The inner mechanisms that, in moments of crisis, led the rest of us to seek emotional support from the group when we couldn't solve a subjective problem alone were missing in him. He seemed never to have understood this great lesson of revolutionary life. On the contrary, he ended by voluntarily cutting himself off, thus sealing his fate.

In another time and under other conditions his fate would surely have been different, but under these circumstances we had no choice. He knew everything about what we had achieved in months of effort and sacrifice, and to allow him to remain alive would have meant putting our lives in his hands, as well as the lives of the villagers who had protected us. We assumed that someone who had not been able to endure the privations of the jungle would surely succumb to torture. We shot him one April morning when many birds were singing. This was one of the world's lovely sounds that he would no longer hear.

We had told him of our decision at a general meeting of our unit. He seemed bewildered, as if he could not believe what he had heard. He then made desperate efforts to save himself. In his desire to live, he promised loyalty and many other virtues; he appealed to the unit as a whole and then to those *compañeros* he felt had the greatest authority, but the expressions on their faces and the answers they gave only confirmed his sentence.

As he walked toward the execution site, he asked for a bit of the sugarloaf he carried in his backpack. As he faced the firing squad he seemed to regain his pride and stood upright during those final moments. A few seconds before the order to fire was given, he attempted a confused speech in which he seemed to call for a rift between Indians and *ladinos*. He refused the blindfold, then turned his face away from the firing squad.

We returned to our posts. A profound silence reigned. The unit had reached maturity. Perhaps from that moment on each of us was a better person.

Six months after entering the country we once again numbered fifteen, because in June Tavo rejoined us. The organization in the city was beginning to grow and his work had made it possible to renew contacts there and set up a logistical support network for our guerrilla force. Now we began to reap the results of our work. At about this time there was a new influx of settlers. In our old stomping grounds we heard everyday noises: the sound of wood being chopped, the shouts of hunters, dogs barking, rifle shots. Along roads we had walked only a week earlier we would come across new clearings, smell the fragrance of wood shavings, and see half-finished beams. This was a time when we would rise at dawn and spend the day

clearing a piece of jungle to help a family—met only the previous day—to settle in. We would help them cut the underbrush,
saw wood, and collect palm fronds for building huts that would
last for ten rainy seasons. Later, when the time came, we would
help plant and tend the first corn. We observed the birds' habits
and the stars' calendar, always watchful of the settlement's needs,
always working, and trying to be responsible.

Our social relationships multiplied rapidly. Whole families
were arriving from remote areas of the country after dangerous
mountain crossings. Many were from the coast, accustomed to
working on plantations, but there were also people from the
east, and above all there were Indians from the different ethnic
groups in the nearby mountains. They arrived with their few
bits of furniture and their pots and pans, followed by one or
two stray dogs. They taught us to calculate where a tree would
fall, how to plant with a digging stick, how to situate a house,
how to find the best wood for the forked poles that supported
the huts, and how to use different kinds of palm leaves for
thatching the roofs that would protect us from the summer's
heat and the torrential rains.

We often found beehives in the trunks of certain trees. If
these were *congo* or *criolla* bees, there was lots of honey, enough
for all. But frequently they were hives from the little *chumelita*
bees, and provided just three or four spoonfuls. In either case,
it meant hours of work to get the honeycombs, and that gave
the guerrilla axe-wielders a chance to demonstrate their skills.
Sometimes these experts could remove the entire comb intact,
first making a difficult lengthwise slash to remove the bark and
reach the wild honey inside the trunk. Redolent of fermented
pollen and wood chips literally covered with bees, they would
victoriously raise their trophy high, rewarded by the applause
of the audience.

Between tasks we found time to teach our neighbors to
read and to use arms, and explained how the October uprising
had come about and what life would be like when the poor governed the world. The first 15th of September—Guatemalan independence day—that we spent in the jungle we put on a political skit, and even those of us who had never made a speech took
the floor. With colored kerchiefs tied around our necks, we pre-

sented arms and raised the flag and sang the national anthem. The villagers improvised a show and provided a feast of tamales. We sang the guerrilla march "Edgar Ibarra," composed by Rigoberto Molina, a *guerrillero* and poet of the previous decade, during the days in the Las Minas mountains:

> Today when our country, cradle of Tecún Umán
> Is governed by thieves and assassins
> The fighters who will guide its destiny
> Are found along the road,
> In the mountains, and in the cities.
> Guatemala, the time has come
> To call your executioners to account.

From that moment on, all of us—villagers and guerrillas—were revolutionary *compañeros*. The man who had begun by talking to us about the Big Dipper and the Little Dipper became our messenger and the man who had asked for advice on bringing a sewing machine up from the coast picked up a gun to start training as a guerrilla. Later on we formed a collective of the best recruits to produce food and share it on the basis of hours worked and need. Part of the harvest was reserved for the guerrillas. Most of the collective's members stopped farming individually and organized their lives around the war of the poor. This experiment in rudimentary communism lasted only until the first enemy attack, but it laid the groundwork for a new kind of social consciousness among those jungle settlers.

That was a time of reunions and separations. Abel arrived, after having been lost for months in Mexico. Sebastián and Atilio left, the first because of illness and the second to reinforce the budding urban organization. Neither was to live long enough to see the first fruits of what he had sown. Edgar stayed on in the village to watch over the cornfields.

We ourselves were not aware of the moment when our consciousness changed, any more than we were aware of the moment when the great change in the seasons took place. When it came time to leave—to go and start a similar cycle in another region—we left behind the best of our lives and our highest hopes. Saturnino, the only guerrilla recruit we obtained in two years, came with us. He imagined that in the mountains he would find an army as vast as our conversations.

THE REGIONS OF THE EAST

Early in 1973 we divided into two groups. One left for the
south, to make its way to the Chamá range; the other went east
to create a base in a village that was then being settled in the
jungle. This group included Alejandro, Jorge, Julián, Abel, and
myself. The village had no name, since the new settlers could
not agree on one. Some called it Santa Cruz del Naranjo and
others simply used the number of the octagon that marked the
site on the map. This was logical, since at that time the entire
village consisted of one communal hut with eight supports and
a thatched roof in a clearing on a small rise on the bank of Río
Tzejá. All kinds of objects and furnishings were piled in the
spacious interior, brought there from more sophisticated areas by
their owners: agricultural implements, scales, metal traps, pots,
chests filled with domestic items, including a mirror with its
silver backing worn away by the heat, which showed us each
time we visited how much we had aged. The villagers had
neither rifles nor a radio; nor had they caught their first parrot
to cheer their lives.

Ramón was the pseudonym of the oldest *compañero* in
the village. He had come from the east and was devoted
to the guerrillas, but he was deeply *machista;* a braggart and
troublemaker of the first order. He never looked you in the eye,
and you could only see their watery yellow color when he
laughed. Once when we surprised him inside the house he remained motionless, as though we had caught him out in some
wrongdoing, in an attitude that reminded us of a wild animal
and certainly did not inspire confidence. But he often invited
us into his home and made us comfortable. He had occasionally
collaborated with the earlier guerrilla movement, and perhaps
because of that was full of false ideas about us. Each time we
chatted he felt obliged to talk of violence and combat. His tales
always led up to the moment when he, brandishing a machete,
had done this or that or the other, or had frightened someone
out of his wits. Once he had a sparrow hawk tied by one leg
to a clothesline. "I'm punishing him," he said with a glint of
satisfaction in his shifty eyes. He kept the bird like that for two
days until it died.

His wife was one of those country women who do not have a moment's rest the entire day. She carried water from the ravine, cooked the corn, ground it, and made the tortillas for the family and for us. At first she became very angry when we took over some of her tasks, but she soon gave in, somewhat amused by the rare spectacle of men grinding corn and patting out tortillas. Although she was small, dark-skinned, and barefoot, her first and last names were those of a Spanish lady, her only legacy from the *ladino* area where she was born. The couple had five daughters, all hard workers and illiterate. They learned to read with us.

Ramón's closest neighbor was a saintly man. He bore the name of a Biblical figure and behaved like one. Meeting us seemed to make him happy. He was very talkative and solicitous. He said meeting us was a "great joy." The phrase struck us and we commented on it among ourselves. It was a significant introduction, to hear those words from such a reserved and upstanding man. He was a bachelor and lived alone in a house near the ravine, eating one day and fasting the next, satisfied for the most part with a bit of squash or some tender root he roasted on the embers and shared with us. He had a large mouth, red as a slice of watermelon, in contrast to his swarthy skin, which was like that of a prophet exiled in the wilderness. Probably heaven rewarded his goodness, because he never lacked for food and constantly praised the miraculous coincidences that supplied him with nourishment. Today it might be the iguana that came to his very door and let itself be killed with a slingshot; yesterday it had been the docile trout that bit the baitless hook. His only friend was a yellow and black jungle bird that visited him from time to time. "Francisquito's here," he would say clasping his hands beatifically. The little bird would enter his hut and light on a beam, where it would sing gaily, hopping about.

We helped him to put the roof on his house since he had not been able to do so for lack of helpers and lived exposed to the rain. As we got to know him, we discovered that for him the work of the guerrillas represented yet another of the many signs of Divine Will, and we soon discovered that "joy" was a common term in his Biblical vocabulary. Almost everything was a "joy" to him. But he fell from grace when, while talking about enemy repression on the coast, he withdrew with a shrug from this secular subject, creating an insurmountable ideological barrier between himself and us. "Well, look," he said, scratching his leg with a twig, "to tell you the truth, I've never had the joy of being garrotted."

The third villager we got to know well was a reserved and agreeable man, sparing of words and gesture. His only sign of life during our conversations were the occasional slaps at mosquitoes and his mechanical nods of agreement. He agreed to everything, and as soon as we began talking politics he would hasten to say yes, even before we could explain that Guatemalans were divided into rich and poor and that the first were called "exploiters" and the second "exploited." "Ah, yes," he would say, slowly advancing a finger toward a blood-gorged mosquito on his arm. "Of course, that's the way it is." He was one of the few who wore shoes. He never showed any interest in the workings of a weapon, and if someone carelessly pointed a gun at him he would calmly move away, without stopping his nods of agreement. Later we learned that much of his character was the result of his occupation: he was a beekeeper, which requires a sweet temper, unlimited patience, and a gentle hand.

That characters such as these could be organized into a local nucleus that would direct the war in the region was an idea that only we could have conceived of.

But there was among them a man and his son who had come from the coast. The father had been a beneficiary of Arbenz's agrarian reform, and was an admirer of the ex-president. A few days after meeting us he brought us some provisions and some crumpled news clips that he had kept for years. One of them showed Arbenz during his presidential campaign, in shirt sleeves, looking very young, talking to a ragged crowd. The posters the group carried—now dimmed with age—bore the letters CNCG, the peasant organization of that time. "He was a brave man," our friend said nostalgically as he studied Arbenz. "Too bad he let himself be thrown out just when things were beginning to get better for us." When the anti-communist reaction regained power in 1954, his plot of land had been snatched away. He still longed for those good old days, and did not lose hope.

We moved around in that area for seven months. The rainy season had just ended and we were feeling the strain of marching for weeks at a time in the great jungle downpour. We had marched from dawn through the tropical rain, soaked to the bone, carrying a recently bagged wild boar, our cartridge cases beginning to swell because of the humidity. That year, anticipating the rainy season, we had built a hut deep in the jungle in early May, and spent the rainy season there. It had posts of *lacandón* wood and a roof of palm thatch, and was near a sandy ravine where wild turkeys often wandered. In that hidden shelter we slowly gathered provisions. It was a time of waiting and planning for the weeks and months ahead. When we were not with the villagers, we spent whole days in camp, working on it, studying, or simply talking. Thus we had time to really get to know each other, since the hard work of the first period had not left us much leisure for exploring each other's inner depths.

Abel, for example, was full of spirit and eager for action. "What would you like today?" he would ask, "a slow-moving biped or a fierce porker?" The old hunters among us, lazing in their hammocks, would look at him, smiling skeptically since they well knew that wild turkey and wild boar aren't easy catches. However, although Abel didn't know the jungle, he was guided by a lucky star and always returned with at least one of the promised game. His best moment occurred once when he had to relieve himself after breakfast, and had the foresight to carry a .22 caliber rifle with him. As luck would have it, at the least appropriate moment an enormous pheasant such as he would never again see decided to cross his path, stretching its elegantly feathered neck and scratching here and there for seeds. Without moving from his squatting position, Abel took aim and with one sure shot downed the black-and-white bird. It was as large as a wild turkey and lasted for three meals.

Despite this striking proof, we never quite believed Abel's stories of his fabulous skill as a hunter in his boyhood. And his hunter's luck failed the day he got lost for the first time. He spent a day and a night wandering in the jungle; for a long time after that he didn't dare go beyond the area where he could hear our radio. Instead he decided to take up his music again. He had brought his guitar with him—the very one that

he had earned his living with, singing on Mexico City buses—
and he offered nightly concerts. His favorite song was "My
Tree and I," but he could pick out "The Condor Is Passing."
At around that time his foot became infected and festered with
maggots, and he had to stay inside while the rest of us went
about our work.

Jorge, another of our group, quickly changed moods. He
was a stalwart *guerrillero* with bushy hair, a heavy beard and
moustache, and slanted eyes that shone with firm determination. "By God," he would suddenly swear, rising from his hammock and preparing to go hunting. "By God, I won't return
until I bring you a deer." Bow-legged and full of energy, he
would wrap the red woven sash of his village around his waist,
pick up a .22 caliber rifle or shotgun, throw his knapsack on
his back, and disappear into the jungle. Five, six, seven hours
would pass. Once in a while, off in the distance, we would hear
a shot; then more hours of silence. He would finally reappear
at dusk, carrying a deer on his back, gaily shouting hurried
orders for the preparation of the roast.

Nevertheless, when Jorge thought about the future, he was
haunted by frightening premonitions. Once, during one of our
criticism–self-criticism sessions, he wept bitterly and confessed
that he had always been frightened of marching at the front of
a column. That outburst led to a discussion about "fate." We
were materialists, and we therefore knew that death is the result
of chance and cannot be foreseen, although one can scientifically
consider it as one of the logical possibilities of war.

When something amused him, Jorge's loud contagious laugh
would ring out, shaking his whole body. A great lover, he spent
his free time writing gallant love letters to one young girl or
another that he met along the way. He had no inhibitions, nor
did he suffer from the deep insecurity that is common to those
who have been victims of discrimination. At our independence
day celebration he sang a solo that he had practiced for a week.
It was a banal love song, but when he sang it, it took on a new
dimension, so pure was the sentiment he expressed.

Julián was a master of patience and a veteran of life.
Working for weeks, he built our first mortar and pestle for hulling rice. He was silent for several days, his hands pressed to his

lips as though he were praying. He was planning his work, and once it had taken shape in his mind he proceeded to carry it out with great efficiency. He took off his shirt, grabbed an axe, and chopped out the heart of a tree trunk. It took several days to carve the double-ended pestle that would be used for pounding the grain, and then he used a torch to burn out the bowl. Weeks later, when he had finished, he undertook the tedious work of hulling rice, from morning till night. It was thanks to his patience that we ate clean rice. While he pounded he would whistle an old Indian tune. He knew how to build and play marimbas. Maybe they reminded him of his son, now growing up in a far away village, whom he had not seen for ten years.

However, he was irritable and easily upset if things went wrong. "You said so, brother," he would say angrily. "You said so with your damned mouth." Later he would criticize himself for his loss of self-control, and would adopt toward his victim the paternal attitude that he assumed toward all of us—except Uncle Pedro who, for reasons of age and rivalry, he always called simply Pedro. Then, an hour after his self-critical session, he would once again be threatening to commit some dreadful act against the Supreme Being.

I got to know Alejo better during the time we went together to find the Río Chixoy. We left in July and wandered for several days, unable to find a way across the Tzejá, trying to catch an armadillo for our supper. "Wait!" he would suddenly say, plunging his arm deep into a hole where the animal hid. "There's a trick to catching armadillos. All you have to do is stick your finger up their ass and they'll hold still."

Alejo talked more with his eyes and with gestures than with words. And he had explosions of rage that he could barely control. He also had a deep prejudice against our *compañeros* who came from petty bourgeois backgrounds, and when he was angry he couldn't hide it. Once when we were building our hut we had disagreed about something, and he didn't know how to handle the situation. His opponent had trapped him in a logical bind, the way someone who has been reading from the age of five can easily do. This exasperated Alejo, particularly since at that age he had been herding goats and making charcoal. Most of the students he had met along the path of revolution had disillusioned him, and he felt justified in mistrusting them. During this unfortunate discussion, he slashed the ground with his machete in anger. Afterward, he vomited until he felt better.

His temper overflowed like a ditch in the rainy season, but at bottom he was a tender person who needed affection. Often he would come to our hammocks, using some pretext or other—a tick was buried in his foot—but really wanting a chance to talk about his childhood, to tell us about the tortillas his mother used to make to earn a little money. He needed to share the hopes and disappointments of his family, which he heard from only every six months or so.

During that trek it became clear that Alejo was extremely suspicious and watchful. We were days away from the nearest populated area, yet he would be on the alert for the slightest sound. He was the first to reach for his gun and load it—a reflex that must have saved his life many times before. At the same time he enjoyed moments of childlike joy, and he laughed with his entire body, gesturing as though to ward off a blow.

We didn't find the river on this trip. Our search ended in an area of huge trees and swampy land where all the jungle's parrots seemed to gather at dusk. Thousands of birds filled that wild and lonely place with a chattering that brought us the greatest happiness.

It was around this time that I saw my first tapir. I was out hunting, thinking how slowly time passed and wondering how to speed it up, when I suddenly saw the legendary beast. Back during our Ixcán days we had found tapir tracks and had often smelled the horsey odor it left along the route it cut with its armored body. At other times we found its excrement, still warm. Neverthless, few of us had seen one—some of us never did. This time I felt I was being watched, and I stood motionless for a few seconds. The tapir, hidden at the bottom of a ravine, was studying me. Judging from the way it stood and its girth, it was probably an old male. I crouched down slowly, trying not to make any noise, and carefully moved into firing position. The tapir watched, unperturbed. When I thought the moment had come to shoot, I fired the first bullet—I was carrying an old .22 caliber Remington. I was concentrating so hard

I almost didn't hear the shot. For a moment I thought the tapir didn't react because the cartridge was wet. I fired again, and although this time I clearly heard the shot, the animal continued to stare at me impassively. I then fired several times in rapid succession. The tapir, as though annoyed by a swarm of mosquitoes, twitched its ears two or three times, slowly turned, and, making the ground tremble with its heavy gait, disappeared into the jungle. For us, I thought, time was like the tapir.

The village was slowly becoming populated, but the months came and went and our message didn't seem to take root in the minds of the villagers. Suspicion, innuendo, and petty disagreements divided the villagers, and gradually each one was shut off in a separate world. The crowing of the rooster in the next yard was all the news one neighbor had of another. Our efforts were dissipated as we too ended by getting involved in these petty disagreements. To resolve each situation, we had to spend an entire week in private meetings with individual villagers. More industriously than ever, we helped them with their gardens and advised them on domestic matters. Then we learned that Ramón had boasted that we trusted him only, that we had named him head of the village, and that they would see what happened when the war began. After a heated meeting at which Ramón was forced to admit his lies, hostilities ceased and the revolution once more set up its invisible government in the village.

Ramón was largely responsible for our setbacks and difficulties, but we also had made mistakes. Since he was the one who demonstrated the most commitment and loyalty to us, we had—and this was one mistake—visited his house more than any of the others. He used our deference toward his family to enhance his status with his neighbors. At one time he even threatened them: we made the mistake of asking him to keep a shotgun for us, and he boasted that this was proof of our support.

We realized how far afield we had gone when a new couple arrived in the village. The first time we met them we gave an aspirin to the young wife, who was suffering from a bad toothache. By our second visit the woman had recovered, and she asked us—just as though were were itinerant traders and not members of the future Army of the Poor—if we didn't have some vaseline and hairpins!

In September we attempted to move south. Our obsession with the highlands had been with us throughout our time in the jungle, and we dreamed of climbing up into the cloudy skies. From Ramón's house we surveyed the horizon and made plans. But between us and the mountain range there was more jungle, well populated, where we had no peasant bases.

The only friendly dwelling was two days' march away, and we decided to head for it. It was the height of the rainy season. The rising of the Río Tzejá took us by surprise and cut off any chance to go back. That day we heard the news of the overthrow of Allende in Chile over the radio. We began our march at dawn, during the worst rainstorm we could remember. Our goal was to obtain supplies from the friendly peasant base and continue marching until they gave out. As we marched in the rain we tried everything to keep dry. A piece of plastic would cover our heads and weapons, but our arms, constantly held above our heads, became channels for the rain to slowly run down our arms and onto our shirts. However, the heat we generated marching kept our clothes warm and we would not become aware of our sodden state until our boots suddenly seemed to weigh too much. Then we realized that we were completely soaked, and would abandon ourselves to the rain. We would stop losing time looking for bridges over the many ravines. Splashing through the water like tapirs, we would cross to the other side, dripping like huge urinating animals. Only the knowledge that when we pitched camp we could change into the dry clothing gave us the strength to endure the weather.

But it had other plans. After ten hours of steady marching, just as dawn broke, and after crossing a bridge that swung over a deep ravine, we were unpleasantly surprised to discover that everything in our packs, including our dry clothes, was soaked through. One single rainstorm washed out two years of our struggle as set down by Alejandro in his diary, and turned our matches into paste. We had to sleep sopping wet, splashing like fish in our hammocks and unable to light a fire. That night we dreamed that we had reached a clearing where we dried our things out in bright sunlight.

Our project failed two days later. We had reached an area where the guerrilla movement had been informed on several times before, and so we tried to reach the foothills without being seen. We crossed some woods silently and ran across a road— only to find that the route we had chosen was through an area that was now densely populated. The foothills that we tried to advance through were full of sawmills and small churches filled with people clapping and singing. We returned, soaked through, defeated by the weather and with our corn sprouting inside our backpacks. We were tied to the jungle like the birds that we had tethered to sticks when we were children.

THE MARCH TO THE MOUNTAINS

In September 1972 we had received our first news from the highlands. Several Indian leaders from San Juan Cotzal had met with us in Ixcán, after learning of our presence there. They were itinerant traders who traveled between the highlands and the jungle villages, and it was not long before our paths crossed. After that first encounter we maintained contact.

In perfect Spanish, learned from the priests and during their frequent trips to the coast, the traders told us about the troubles in their village. Five years earlier, the guerrillas of the previous period had visited the northwest area for the first time. It seems that those who had been preparing for war back then had hoped to develop a supply route from the highlands to the jungle. They walked openly along the highway, did not carry machetes—and thus were easily detectable. When they visited people's houses they did not carry out any political work. They paid generously for supplies and help. They were frequently denounced to the authorities by the peasants. After their fleeting appearances, they would vanish. We met a family that, five years later, was still waiting for the return of those guerrillas. They had hidden some clothes that they had bought for one of these groups, and they were still saving them.

The situation in Cotzal had reached a boiling point with the execution of Jorge Brol, a landowner who had built up his estate by plundering the countryside and robbing the peasants. Although some felt his end was justified, most did not understand the reasons for it, because the execution was not followed by a political explanation, or any other kind of political activity. In fact, many people believed that he had been killed during a hold-up.

Some of the Ixil leaders who had participated in the action against Brol fled to the more populated coast, while others remained in hiding. One of the leaders, Domingo Sajic, was captured months later on a coastal plantation. After being brutally tortured by the military police, he was taken back to Cotzal and thrown into a coffee drier on the Brol's San Francisco plantation. But the repression did not stop the discontent and hatred of the rich from growing.

In December 1973, a year after the capture, we began our march to the mountains. All we had to guide us were the directions our Cotzal friends had given us and marks on a map. The time had come at last for us to ascend into the Indian world. Lacho had been the first of us to embark on this venture, and had left months before to open up an initial route into the highlands. Mario had followed him a few months later. By June we had managed to set up a camp on a rocky ridge in the foothills, a cool spot thick with ferns and other tropical plants. It was on the tropical side of the mountain range, and was lashed by the strong highland winds. The water in the streams was crystal clear and plunged swiftly through crevasses in the rocks. There we saw Ju again. She was the first *compañera* to have gone into the mountains.

A few days after setting up camp we discovered that we were sitting on the ruins of an ancient Indian city. We even dug up an ancient grinding stone, polished by the centuries. When we explored more carefully, we found other remains. The bed of the ravine behind the camp was paved with stones that had been cut and placed in neat rows. The stream ran into the ravine between ancient walls, now covered with moss. Looking up, we could see the mountains looming up into the clouds.

As we climbed, the vast expanse of the jungle receded in the distance, and within a few days the din of the jungle had been left far behind. After climbing another mile or so, there were no more wild turkey hens flying by. At this point the trail ended and we entered the mist. We marched through silent, damp areas where no birds sang. After scaling a sharp cliff covered with mountain palms, we reached the top. It was a dry area, covered with old trees bearded with long strands of Spanish moss.

December brought freezing weather, but because of the dampness we could build fires only with the cores of tree trunks. The bright-colored heavy woolen knitted caps worn by the highland Indians became indispensable items of clothing. The only comfortable place in camp was close to the fire. If we moved only a few steps away from it, the cold numbed our very bones and the mist soaked us through. Using pieces of plastic, we collected and saved the rain water, the only way of obtaining drinking water at this height. We decided to take medicine for parasites, and for almost a whole week we excreted the millions of worms that had invaded our bodies in the tropics. But we did free ourselves somewhat from the constant hunger that we had felt in the jungle and for a while our appetites were normal. In a few weeks we had become acclimated to the altitude.

December is the time for oranges in the mountains, so once again we could enjoy that civilized fruit. The oranges were brought to us by Indians from the Cuchumatanes mountains who visited for a few days and entertained us with many unforgettable stories of the remote villages of Huehuetenango where from time immemorial people had trapped birds to eat because of the extreme poverty of the land and the gradual fragmentation of their properties. Some of our visitors were old and had heard from their grandparents the history of exploitation and forced labor during the time of Rufino Barrios, president from 1873 to 1885. The father of one of our visitors had shared the sufferings of those Indians who had built the highland railway.

Two Indian youths who spoke the Mam language stayed with us as we crossed the mountains. They were evangelical Protestants and fine singers, so that when they returned to their village they sang of the good news of the guerrillas, accompanying themselves on their guitars.

At this point, our supply route lengthened. We were in a

sparsely inhabited area where we had only scattered bases, each far from the next. The intense cold and the huge amount of energy required to march across difficult terrain made it necessary to consume large amounts of sugar and calories. We would often make day-long marches uphill, followed by day-long marches downhill. When we would at last reach a mountaintop, two or three more would appear ahead of us. We were in a cold forested area where it was practically impossible to hunt and the few households we came across did not produce a surplus, so that our food problem once again became acute. For more than two months we had to get our supplies from markets in an area where all the inhabitants knew each other and we ran the constant risk of being reported to the authorities. Rumors about us began to spread, but the popular imagination magnifies everything relating to guerrillas, so the people we met in the market or on the road never imagined that these flesh-and-blood men with packs on their backs were the heroes of the legends that were circulating. We were thus able to cross the most inhospitable forests in the country without the villagers' knowledge.

Meanwhile, many of the principles that were to mark the slow creation of revolutionary bases began to emerge as we made contact with these people. We began to understand the proud indifference of so many of the inhabitants of the Indian regions. The language barrier and the ancient mistrust of *ladinos* were, of course, factors, but these did not explain how we had been able to establish contact with the Ixil leaders and with the other Indians we had met in recent months. The answer lay, as always, in their different material conditions.

One afternoon, months later, at the mouth of the Río Copón, we met two Nebaj Indians, father and son, carrying slingshots. They lived an hour's walk from there and were out hunting birds. They answered our greeting from afar, then disappeared into the woods. A little later we heard the distinctive calls that the highland people use to communicate. They had probably separated to check their traps and were telling each other their whereabouts. The next day we found their family dwellings, two or three log and palm-thatch huts, blackened on the inside by the smoke of their hearths. In the trampled earth yard, the women sat on their haunches weaving their intricately decorated cloth while the men fixed the squirrel traps.

This was a self-sufficient family unit, many hours' walk from the nearest market. The members of the previous generation had arrived in the forest looking for land. They had chopped down the bush on either side of the river and over the years had created the basis for their subsistence economy, now carried on by their descendants. They grew corn in the fields, a little sugarcane and a few bananas around the huts, and other grain and squash between the rows of corn. They made most of their tools and utensils themselves. Salt, an occasional axe, and a machete were the only items they bought in the market with the money raised from the sale of the rattan they gathered in the mountains.

Their livelihood influenced their psychology and produced a simple vision of the world. To them, people did not differ from each other because of their material goods, but because of their different languages and customs. Thus plantation owners were from a different lineage, they were *ladinos*. They had had no contact with poor *ladinos,* since where they lived there were only other Indians—the existence of only two or three surnames in the area indicated how closely knit they were. Far from the world of commodities, money had only a relative value for them. And since they knew only a small piece of reality, they were involved with the particular and had difficulty understanding the general. War seemed to them to be as inexplicable and incongruous as the typhus epidemics that had once devastated their villages.

The beginning of 1974 found us almost 9,000 feet above sea level, stiff with cold and losing hope of ever reaching the populated regions. A week earlier we had crossed an uninhabited forest where for the first time we saw quetzal birds in flight. Although we used maps, distances always proved far greater than anticipated: what seemed on the map to be hours away turned out to require several days' march. Around that time the radio told us about the Kohoutek Comet—according to the news, this was the major astronomic event of the century. By coincidence, we were about to climb the highest peak on our route. For four days we traveled through an area barren except for lichen and moss. For drinking water we had to squeeze out the dew these plants had collected. Two attitudes became apparent among us, symbolized in Spanish literature by Don Quixote and Sancho Panza. The Quixotes—the idealists—proclaimed that they wanted to remain overnight on the peak to await the comet. The Sanchos announced that there was no reason to spend any more time in that lonely spot, and that they were going on before the cold got any worse. They hastily clambered down a ravine, searching for a river we could hear several hours below.

Starting in the early morning, those of us who had decided to stay set to work cutting deep into the moss until we came to solid ground. We made a thick mattress of pine needles and covered it with an improvised plastic tent. We built a fire in front of our observatory to act as a reflector, and commenced scrutinizing the sky. Since we did not know the comet's position, we searched the sky with our binoculars, but to no avail. To the south, far away, we could make out the volcanic range of the Sierra Madre; to the east, almost overhead, the frozen ethereal Cuchumatanes. We had heard that the comet would be visible in broad daylight, because of the closeness of its passage to the earth. Later we learned that it did not have the anticipated spectacular features—something to do with the solar light and the chemical composition of the comet's tail. It was only after we had given up our search that we saw it, purely by chance. One of us, busy poking the fire, saw the luminous tail out of the corner of his eye. It was due west, the sun was already down and the first stars had appeared. In honor of this experience, we named the peak where we camped Kohoutek. (We gave the same name to the first shipment of arms, which arrived from the city a few weeks later.) The next day, scarcely an hour's march away, we found the spot where our *compañeros* had pitched camp. They had not reached the river as they had planned, blocked by a barrier of dense vegetation.

Some days later we entered the first villages. We had at last arrived at the populated Indian areas, with their ethnic complexities and innumerable roads. We were in a world completely governed by the laws of commerce, and we soon discovered that the principal consequence of these laws was annual migration. The Indians' landholdings had been fragmented over the generations and the soil was exhausted from having borne crop after crop. Forced off their ancient land and into the mountains during the Spanish conquest, the forebears of today's Indians had stubbornly resisted their oppression, protected by the difficult terrain and their own isolation. They refused to learn the language of the conquerors and adapted Catholic ritual to their own forms of worship. Their frequent revolts were put down by fire and sword, and after years of exploitation by governments and landowners, their communal lands—deeded them by the Spanish Crown—had been reduced to tiny plots on the outskirts of the larger villages, with a few scattered elsewhere in the area.

The corn-growing cycle took almost a year. It required a great deal of work and several different systems of cultivation according to the composition of the soil. For the great majority, the harvest was barely enough for a few months. After that, money for buying corn was obtained by migrating to the coastal plantations. There the Indians picked coffee and cotton, cut cane, and returned to the village for the feast day, speaking Spanish, dressed like *ladinos,* and just as poor as when they left. Their free time was spent working at a craft—braiding hemp, weaving hats, making fireworks. In the towns, this was often done at night, because the artisans could take advantage of the street lights. During the migration period the villages were empty. The spinning wheel, the loom, and the agricultural implements remained inside the huts, unused, and the huts themselves were shut while their owners were away.

This human anthill quickly had a good effect on our lives. Our underground members had been working in the area for several months, so that we got regular shipments of food sent to our camp. This division of labor left us more time for our political talks with, and military training of, the many people who were beginning to know about us. We were inexperienced in dealing with large numbers of people, however, and so we made many mistakes. Too often we financed the real or supposed needs of our new *compañeros,* thus generating material self-interest. Furthermore, we continued in the mistaken practice of putting the new organization under the authority of their own leaders, although their ways of thinking blocked the expansion of the war.

But we soon realized that the poor had to finance their own war, and that the most resolute and politically aware among them should be its leaders. The roads to revolution are numerous and we were just beginning to tread them.

All of our ideas about this were contained in the rudimentary draft of our military strategy that we had worked out along our march. In truth it was more a rough outline of the war, whose main purpose was to understand how we could gain strength in the mountains, thus converting the entire guerrilla territory into an impregnable bastion. It paid more attention to military maneuvers than to the humans who would have to carry out all these feats. We still did not fully understand all the connections between the economic structure and war. According to our document, war arises out of an explosive situation, a violent confrontation between antagonistic social classes, but is regulated and directed. We had neither delved deeply into the Indians' dual condition, exploited and oppressed, or into their dual aspirations. Above all, we had overlooked the fact that for the great machine of war to move, the motor of clandestine organization had to be set in motion.

Many of these ideas became clear during the first guerrilla conference we organized in the mountains. It was a memorable event during which we gave a name to our organization, defined its structure, and officially set up a national directorate. The group that had to split up in Mexico was reunited. One morning, transformed by their journey across that world of quetzals and mocking birds, Rolando and Felipe appeared. A few days earlier, Manolo had arrived. Thus, after many setbacks, the mountains reunited us. Before separating once again, we held many productive work sessions in which we minutely analyzed the formative period and laid our plans for the future. almost to the time when we would take power. We also found the time to recount our experiences during the long separation.

As frequently happens at such moments, we penetrated the farthest reaches of memory.

Rolando turned out to have had extaordinary adventures and a complicated itinerary. Ten years earlier, for example, when he disembarked at Caxlampón to attempt the first guerrilla incursion into the Las Minas range, he had seen what few of the region's inhabitants ever saw: a manatee, that strange sea mammal that the sailors of antiquity took to be sirens, dining by moonlight on the succulent algae at the river's bank. Even earlier, during his flight into exile in Argentina, some time around 1945, one of the plane's engines had died, and the group of Guatemalan exiles on board had indulged in typical black humor about life and death and thrown bottles of whiskey and their own gear overboard. Later, in the jail where Perón had hospitably lodged them, an unknown young woman had appeared with the gift of a book. She explained that the Argentine Communist Youth wanted to let the exiles know the solidarity of the Argentinian people, and she had been chosen by lot to bring them that simple present. Her name was Tita Infante. She turned out to be the girlfriend that unkempt young Argentinian adventurer had told Rolando about during his months of asylum in the Argentinian Embassy in Guatemala. That young fellow would in time be known to the world as Ernesto Che Guevara.

As we obtained more weapons, we also gained new recruits. Among them were Bonifacio and Tino, the first two Ixil youths to take up arms, Haroldo—the very first of all the recruits—Armando, Carlos, and Guillermo, all of whom came from the city and the southern coast. This group of young men brought with them the joyousness of youth and the logic proper to their age. In the midst of a serious discussion at the evening meetings, they would suddenly burst into irreverent laughter or inopportune farts. We would then have to analyze the contradictions inherent in mirth.

We also had to explain over and over again our views regarding possessions, which had been developed during the preceding period. The young men's first battles were waged against the mice that plundered the camp's food supplies—but more than once it turned out that the looters were not exactly rodents. However, in time the mountains matured them and they became excellent *guerrilleros*. Only one, Guillermo, a Pocom Indian, never took root. He returned to the city and left the organization. He went to work in a factory and was killed during a series of protests in October 1978 in a battle at a barricade.

From this point on our tasks multiplied rapidly. The news that an army of the poor was being formed in the Quiché mountains spread and many villages asked us to come to them. One week the camp took on the appearance of a carnival, with men who arrived wrapped in woolen blankets and carrying little harmonicas, come to hear about the revolution. When the discussions reached a difficult point about land ownership or how taxation would be handled in the new society, they chattered in their own dialect and settled down only when the point was completely clear. A week later our visitors went home, full of new ideas, while we in turn found our language enriched by Guatemala's most ancient words.

And despite the fact that the "secret" of our existence was known throughout the region, the enemy never found out. Ethnic barriers helped us keep our secret, and no information leaked out.

The veterans of Ixcán, those of us who had lived through the days of the jungle and whose weapons had rusted in rainstorms and river crossings, finally had to cut our hair, change our guerrilla garments for civilian clothes, and take the road toward the villages armed only with revolvers and a few rudimentary ideas about how to organize the people.

At around that time one of the older guerrillas heard birds sing in his heart when he met a *compañera* who had come from the city to spend a few days, carrying a slate and alphabet cards, with which she was to teach the young illiterates who had taken up arms to read. Sandra arrived and Jacobo returned from the city, where he had gone to get treatment for a shotgun wound in his foot. A few days later Claudio and Lucas arrived as well. Nevertheless, when we left the area, the permanent members of our group could almost be counted on the fingers of both hands. But like a ripening peach tree, we were losing our blossoms and beginning to bear fruit.

THE JAGUAR OF IXCAN

In the spring of 1975 the different guerrilla units converged in the jungle. By then the organization had spread through the mountains over an area of more than 800 square miles. The original detachment, like a beehive, had multiplied, creating two or three armed units. But these units had no true cohesion or combat experience—during the past twenty-six months we had taken only one shot at the enemy, even though there were almost fifty men under arms. A constant stream of peasants sought out our local cells, bringing with them their ancient burden of grievances. Their desperation was in part the result of the new awareness we had brought to them. Popular pressure for action was strong, but the lack of imminent combat was part of our political work. Naturally, the number of people willing to fight far surpassed the number of weapons, even counting shotguns.

This rapid growth in a sense hurt us qualitatively. Our presence was a secret known to thousands, and so much preparation and bustle had not gone unnoticed by the enemy. We expected the first offensive against our guerrilla territory at any moment. We knew we were building on sand. It was not possible to continue building an organization planned for war in peaceful circumstances. The lack of military action was resented throughout the country. Our organization in the city, despite initial success, had not prospered and was running in circles, unable to find the path leading to the masses. On the southern coast implantation work was barely under way, despite many attempts to create an underground structure. All over the country our units discussed the way out of that labyrinth of contradictions in March. Our own discussions in the jungle led to the first campaign plan for the highlands. Its central objective—which was to be duplicated across the country—was to launch a limited military operation, limited so that the enemy's reaction would not exceed either what the people were prepared to understand or what we were capable of withstanding and defending at the local level. The wind we set in motion should not be so strong as to strip the blossoms from the tree. Our military force was therefore not to act as a unit, but to divide into three parts and begin with armed propaganda actions. In this way, the organization would enter a new phase of development, which we would be able to judge the enemy's ability to respond to. We thus split into three detachments, each with its own zone of operations. Those of us who left to take part in the highlands operation had as our first task the punishment of one of the area's most hated landowners, Luis Arenas Barrera, better known as the Jaguar of Ixcán.

The Ixcán jungle is famous for its jaguars. This extraordinarily beautiful and ferocious animal is seen only occasionally, although the peasants of the area frequently suffer from its forays. Its strength and agility are legendary. Pork being its favorite meat, it is said that once a great jaguar carried off an adult male hog weighing 200 pounds, jumping over the pen's fence with it. A great hunter, the jaguar's movements are perfectly coordinated. One reportedly carried off several dogs in a series of stealthy raids that were not noticed until the following morning. The mating season begins in December. When a hunter sounds his horn, the male's answering roar can be heard in the distance. A few moments later, the crashing of broken branches indicates he is near. When he responds to love's call, he loses all sense of caution.

The courageous wife of one of the peasants faced a jaguar alone one night. Hearing noises in the hut where the pigs were kept, she took a lantern and went to investigate. Alerted by the noise of her movements, the jaguar had leaped into the rafters seconds before she entered. He remained crouched in the darkness, but the gleam of his eyes betrayed him. Quickly closing the door behind her, the woman went for her absent husband's rifle. She returned, entered the hut, took aim, and killed the animal. In the stillness of death, out of its natural environment, the jaguar's body resembles the abandoned disguise of an evil jungle spirit. Its loose jaws reek of carrion.

It was our mission to punish Luis Arenas Barrera, whose cruelty and total lack of feeling had led the peasants to call him the Jaguar of Ixcán. Luis Arenas owned a farm that he frequently visited on the banks of the Río Xaclbal, in the mountains where the river separates the central massif of the Cuchumatanes from the wooded mountains of northern Quiché. His notoriety dated back to the days of the U.S. intervention in 1954 when the new government gave him the farm. It was cleared and built upon the backs of the Indians from the highlands. Entire groups of peons were recruited with all sorts of promises and taken to clear the jungle. Many of the workers were transported in military helicopters and left to their fate for months on end. Some tried to escape by walking through the jungle, but, without weapons or food, most died in the attempt. On some of his land, the Indians were put into stocks.

On one of Arenas' holdings, La Perla, most of the peons were "working off" endless debts. Arenas would give them advances on their small coffee crops and then collect in kind at extortionate rates. The coffee beans were carried on mule trails to the larger towns. His strongmen, on horseback, cleared the way at gun point. His name was associated with violence and desecration.

We started the march to the Arenas domain in the last week of April. Our plan was to approach surreptitiously so that he would not flee. The success of this operation was crucial to the successful launching of our military operations in the highlands, as well as throughout the country. Most of our unit's members were new recruits, lacking military experience and enough arms. They hoped to acquire both, but they had no real sense of how hard these were to come by. The minor ordeals of the early stages of the march revealed the frailty of their convictions and the long road that still had to be covered in their political training. It was midsummer and there was no water in the mountains. The day before, trying to quench their thirst, they had eaten raw fruit and had suffered from stomach cramps. After three days' march, they began to become demoralized.

Our destination was still several days' march away, across more arid and uninhabited mountains. The afternoon that the first sign of mutiny appeared, we decided to find a village, stock up on water, and shorten the march by walking along the main road at night. It was the only way to avoid a crisis without giving up our goal. But our hopes quickly faded. There was no water in the village. The only well was several miles away, and was a veritable pigsty. That night on the main road we covered a distance that would have taken us several days along mountain trails. At midnight, exhausted and obsessed by thirst, we had to make do with a puddle where animals came to drink. We removed the slimy crust and found a thick liquid that many of our group drank to the bursting point. At dawn the veterans among us carried the weapons for the others, who were on the verge of giving in to fatigue and refusing to go on. Our safety limit for walking on the road was 5:00 A.M., when the first early risers appear. Yet daylight found us on open ground, still some distance from the mountains. We had to spend the day a few steps off the road, crouched in the bushes, listening to the voices of the passersby. At nightfall we moved to the only spring in the area, inside the forest, and set up camp for several days.

For the new recruits the war ended there. Two or three days later they all found various pretexts for returning home. Since none of them knew our plans, we let them go. We parted on good terms, remembering the law of the jungle regarding the rhythm of war and the seasons, but the experience disappointed us deeply. That afternoon we understood that if they had no idea of the significance of the first battle, we were far from understanding the complexities of the war. In order to produce honey the pollen has to be carefully chosen and the wax hive carefully built to await the time of its great qualitative transformation. We were the bees and the war was the honey; the hive was our organization.

Meanwhile our camp had a splendid arsenal of .22 caliber rifles and single-barrel shotguns that had to remain buried until better days came. Our unit was reduced to eight stalwarts, some of whom were laid low by the malaria we had brought with us from the lowlands. Because of a last-minute mistake, our anti-malaria medicine had remained in the backpack of a *compañero* who was no longer in our unit. This greatly multiplied the work of the healthy: in order to bring us the only vial of quinine in the region, two of the best Ixil hikers had to cover sixty miles in three days.

After a month of such hardship, we were a group of skeletons chasing the few rays of sunlight that filtered through the dense foliage. Then the rains came and it begun to thunder.

The last days of May were spent in exploring and gathering the information necessary for the execution. Aware of his own record of atrocities, and knowing there were guerrillas in the jungle, Arenas moved with extreme caution, following no fixed route or schedule. Sometimes he arrived by plane and sometimes on horseback. Even his physical appearance varied according to the fear—and imagination—of his describer.

His home base, La Perla, was a fortress. It was perched on a high promontory, impossible to reach unseen. The bare foot-hills of the Cuchumatanes protected it to the west. It was always in contact with the outside world by radio. Because of all this we decided to watch for Arenas on the road, dressed as civilians and using small arms. Since we had only three pistols, we sent messengers to our nearest local base, two days away, for appropriate weapons. They returned with a memorable arsenal: three rusty, battered objects, one of which the old Indians called a harquebus, which was not the long weapon used by the Spaniards, but a kind of antique musket.

Never will the maps we relied on for carrying out our operation be equaled in the annals of war. Our mapmakers had recently learned to write and their fingers were still unused to holding a pencil. Resembling the maps of the ancient explorers, they included every accident of nature and described every site and custom, a fat-cheeked sun to the west and a fanciful rose symbolizing the winds. They could be read either way up, since they had been drawn with a childlike sense of perspective. Nevertheless, we could follow on them our route of approach and return.

But after one unsuccessful ambush on the road, we decided to surprise our quarry in his own fortress. June 7 was pay day, *1975* which made it easier for us to approach the offices where the workers were to collect their wages. They clustered in front of the manager's office waiting for their money. Standing in front of the manager and looking like a bird of prey, the lord of the land was counting his coins and unfolding some crumpled bills. When we ordered him to raise his hands, his eyes rested for a second on his assailants and he instinctively reached for his gun. A quick burst of gunfire killed him just as he was pressing the trigger of his revolver.

Not believing what they had just seen, the crowd nervous-
ly listened to the explanation, in their own language, that we
offered then and there. As the indictment progressed, recalling
Arenas' injustices and depredations, voices began to be heard
among the crowd, interrupting the speaker and adding justifi-
cations of their own for the man's execution. Finally shouts of
joy burst from throats accustomed for centuries only to silence
and lament, and with something like an ancestral cry, with one
voice they chanted with us our slogan, "Long live the poor,
death to the rich."

We did not take one *centavo* of the money scattered on
the table and floor. From that moment on, the word spread
throughout the region that the guerrillas were not foreigners
since they spoke the local dialect, that they were not thieves,
since they hadn't touched the money, and that they had surely
come to do justice, since they had punished a man who had
grown rich from the blood and sweat of the poor.

Two days of fiesta in Ilóm, a neighboring village, was the
best proof of the people's joy over the event. When we later
visited some isolated settlements, many of the Indians—above
all the elderly—took our hands and looked long into our eyes
in gratitude.

The news of the death of the Jaguar of Ixcán at the hands
of Indian guerrillas spread rapidly throughout the mountains.
The first shots of the people's war had been heard. The next
day the sky was dark with helicopters and military planes. During the following months the enemy unleashed the heaviest anti-
guerrilla operation the country had yet seen. Hundreds of
soldiers were parachuted from old C-47's into Ixcán settlements
and columns penetrated by land from different military bases,
occupying key points in the jungle. They were waiting to hear
our gunfire before they landed in full force.

They installed themselves in the main town and from there
troops trained for jungle combat combed the mountains. For
three months they took over the roads and searched the villages,
arresting anyone who seemed suspicious or who was listed in
their intelligence files. The entire guerrilla territory fell within
the enemy's blockade.

After the operation at La Perla, our patrol retreated without mishap to a distant jungle region. From that point on, communication with our *compañeros* in the lowlands was cut off. The roads were thick with soldiers, and radio newscasts and the remote buzzing of helicopters were our only sources of information.

THE GUERRILLAS COME OF AGE

The first effects of the enemy offensive were felt immediately by our group in the jungle. One morning, when the threatening hum of enemy planes could be heard in the distance to the south of us, a young lieutenant accompanied by a large troop of soldiers turned up at the home of our oldest collaborator. He asked for the owner of the house and for information about the roads. The house belonged to David, a remarkable old man who, although over 60, had maintained the high spirits and strength of his youth. He was heavy set, with skin weathered by a lifetime in the open air, the strong hands of a woodcutter, and the wisdom of one who has learned the ways of the world through his work. He could name on sight numerous species of timber trees, knew by heart the life cycles and secrets of the basic human foods, and even knew all about bees, rainfall, and plant grafting.

When he was about nineteen he had been one of those who, with rifle and ammunition, awaited the call to arms against the dictator Manuel Estrada Cabrera. He would recall tenderly his childhood home on the coast, with its patio filled with banana trees and rosebushes, where plovers marked the hours. He remembered as though it was yesterday the bands of coatis and flocks of parrots moving through the boundless spaces of the Pacific Coast when the area was still virgin jungle only beginning to be penetrated by the railroad. He would go from one plantation to the next, his father holding him by the hand, helping clear land for the benefit of the large landowners who brought their herds of cattle into the meadows that had been cleared by the peasants. He had vivid memories of a sawmill in the forest where he had learned about the trees, and of the time he went into town and first saw that new invention, the train. In his youth he knew all the popular songs and when asked would sing in a young man's voice the melody that the early food vendors used to sing at the railroad stations:

> Sweet cakes, sesame seed, *pupusas* with cheese
> Fried fish, cheap, a peso apiece
> Please buy, sir, my delicious marzipan
> My fried fish from [Lake] Amatitlán.

While the lieutenant and David talked, sizing each other up, more on the basis of gestures and looks than on the few phrases they exchanged, the soldiers took stock of the surroundings. The lieutenant seemed about to go, and then suddenly changed his mind. Very courteously, he asked David to prepare a chicken for lunch. Later he said goodbye and left with his men on the road they had come by. The following day a new group of soldiers appeared, but this time they caught him by surprise, arriving from the opposite direction; without further ado they took David prisoner. He repeatedly denied having any links with the guerrillas and had perfect alibis, but he was in any case handcuffed, thrown to the ground, and, while his sons watched, beaten unconscious. "Be a man and kill me once and for all, but don't leave me crippled," he said to the officer who was beating him.

David was president of the settlement and a man of recognized integrity; it was perhaps because of this that the soldiers were afraid to kill him. They left him there, more deeply wounded by the affront to his dignity than by the blows, although several ribs were broken. His youngest son helped him to his feet, then watched him suddenly walk away, trembling, silent, as though he had lost his wits and his bearings. That night his sons brought his rifle to him and he spent the rest of the army's offensive hidden in the mountains.

Other *compañeros* were less fortunate than David. They were picked up by the enemy in the fields or at home, in full daylight or in the middle of the night. They were savagely beaten and taken to the local command post. One heavy-set sergeant, made to order for the job at hand, would smash the men's faces until they fell unconscious, bathed in blood. When forcing bamboo splinters under their fingernails failed to make them break their silence, they were shot without further ado, or dropped from helicopters. These planes, flying just above the treetops, thundered over the villages.

Peasants who ventured out on the road and trails would suddenly be ordered to halt and lie face down while a military unit passed. The commanders, potbellied and sweaty, would hurry by, barking out orders and complaining of the discomforts of the job. The barking of dogs would announce some midnight capture in a hamlet. Pointing their guns at the women and children, the soldiers would make the adult males come out of the huts. They were never seen again. Terror began to spread. Just as jungle birds scatter when a jaguar appears in a clearing, so many of our peasant bases managed to disappear when the army appeared. In less than a week we tripled our membership, augmented by the peasants who sought our protection. Four or five different dialects were suddenly heard in our camps. Other peasants took the road back to their home villages, never to return. Many of those who took up arms during this offensive—particularly those who had thought about it for years—did so fully aware of what they were doing. They took the time to arrange domestic details with their wives and with deliberation took up their rifles. Others, however, arrived at our camps with their hearts still pounding violently. These were the ones who turned pale and started trembling at the mere sound of a helicopter in the distance.

A few had the good fortune to escape from their captors. Lorenzo, a Mam Indian and the father of a large family, was held captive for nearly two months. All that time he defended himself against his accusers with arguments grounded in religious conviction. His ribs were broken with pistol butts, and he was made to eat green plantains and threatened with drowning in the river if he didn't talk. One morning while he was chopping wood for the kitchen fire, he managed to escape into the jungle. He wandered for several months near the Mexican border, doing occasional agricultural work. As soon as possible, he returned to his home region and reestablished contact with our organization.

On the other hand, Ernesto, a Quiché soothsayer, was held for only a few hours. When he was being taken to a command post, marching along the edge of a ravine, he took advantage of the fact that the attention of the soldier behind him in the column wandered for a moment and he sped into the jungle. He hid there for several days, eating roots and spending the nights hidden in the treetops.

In spite of the enemy's offensive, our forces did not loose the initiative. While repression was wreaking havoc in the western part of the area, our two military units in the jungle joined forces and took several villages in the east. Two enemy agents, notorious in the area, were captured and executed. After we took a village we would gather the peasants in the village center and explain the reasons for our struggle. We also gave them suggestions for defending themselves against the army. Hundreds of peasants received our message during that armed propaganda campaign. The peasants learned to their amazement that we *guerrilleros* were people just like them, armed, of course, as well as possible, and speaking of victory with so much conviction that our hopes were contagious. We denounced the army's atrocities and their looting of the peasants' property—wherever they went, the soldiers carried off chickens and any other food they could find. After one of these lengthy meetings we would accept donations of grain and tortillas offered spontaneously by the people, who often risked being informed on. Afterward, our group of armed peasants would suddenly disappear into the jungle.

But the jungle was no longer the impenetrable refuge it had once been. The anti-guerrilla forces, spurred on by their officers, moved deep into the area, persistently searching for signs of our presence. They made so much noise as they advanced that they alerted our forces, allowing us to move on quickly. But no site was safe: small enemy patrols, moving cautiously and leaving almost no tracks, scoured the jungle, listening for any sound or clue that would lead them to us. They had radio transmitters and immediately informed their command posts of anything unusual. We therefore limited ourselves to advancing only when absolutely necessary. We were careful not to return to former campsites, since the enemy checked them again and again.

In absolute silence, our packs on our backs, we would spend the daylight hours studying, always with an eye on the nearest cover. More than once we watched as enemy troops marched by, and heard the shouted orders and general clamor characteristic of military units on the move. On other occasions, however, the enemy's scouts took us by surprise. This happened to one patrol that was to evacuate a family that had aided us. After carefully exploring an old site and finding no signs of the enemy, the patrol pitched camp at nightfall. The *compañero* in charge, one of the founders of our original detachment, a calm man with a highly developed sense of vigilance, took the first watch, on the alert for the family, which was expected to arrive at the camp momentarily. He had just taken up his post when he heard steps behind him. At first he thought it must be one of his *compañeros,* but he instinctively turned around—just as several enemy soldiers appeared. Without losing a second, without even getting into firing position, he opened fire, felling one soldier instantly. Then he spotted the commanding officer, who had taken cover behind a tree and had begun firing his automatic. Our *compañero* aimed at the man, but the trigger jammed. He took off quickly, dropping his machete and beret in the process.

When the enemy began firing the leaves shook, and our *compañero* took refuge in a shallow depression in the ground. Leaves and small branches rained down on him, shaken loose by the bullets that were destroying the foliage above. He scouted the area during the night and at dawn, his nerves on edge, he had yet another stroke of bad luck. He stepped on a coiled *mazacuata* snake. But by afternoon he had rejoined his patrol group in the main camp. The peasant family—a couple and their five daughters—who should have been evacuated had had to leave on their own. They wended their way through the jungle for a week, evading the army's anti-guerrilla blockade, and managed to avoid meeting any soldiers.

Far from our base, our supply routes cut off by enemy encirclement, those were difficult days. Once our small reserves of food were used up, we had to obtain our food directly from the fields. However, the enemy kept close watch over the peasants' plots as part of their siege, and the forays we were forced to make into the cornfields frequently ended in skirmishes. Frequently too, we would return empty-handed, although we never suffered any casualties. As for us, we always wounded or killed at least one of the enemy. But as time passed our food situation worsened, and we had to resort to gathering berries and eating mountain palm. This hastened the crisis for many of the refugees who had come to us for protection. If they had had to choose between torture and death at the hands of the enemy and hunger in our camps, many would have chosen the first. We thus had to watch for the enemy with one eye and keep the other on possible mutineers among the refugees.

The caution that characterized our *compañeros* movements is exemplified by the following anecdote. Two of our youngest members, out looking for palmshoots at dusk, saw some in a clearing. They advanced so cautiously that a jaguar scratching the ground did not hear them approach. All three stared at each other for a long time until the animal turned and trotted off into the jungle.

On several occasions, while the rest of the guerrillas carried out tasks far from camp, our women *compañeras*—one of whom was so nearsighted she could scarcely make out shapes ten yards away—kept the troublemakers at bay. The slightest concession would have been fatal for us. Our political work redoubled and discipline was tightened. Absolute silence was ordered in the camps, and a schedule set up for absolutely necessary activities. Fires were lit after dark, but only after careful reconnoitering.

Soon, though, we had some good news. Saturnino and Rodolfo, who had been lost for several weeks, reappeared safe and sound. They had spent all that time in one of the villages where we had a popular base of support and where the enemy's offensive had subsided. A few days later, we moved our camp near the cornfields and awaited the first crop. It was August, harvest time. Helicopter flights were down to routine periodic sorties and the enemy returned to its barracks. The first great offensive against the jungle had ended. Although the guerrillas in the mountains suffered no losses, these were considerable among our organized supporters in the villages. Beloved *compañeros* who had reached out and supported us from the first were buried in the jungle. Perhaps reincarnated as lemon trees on a small farm, they watched us pass, content in the knowledge that we were pursuing the cause to which they gave their lives.

The main lesson we learned from this offensive was the

need for organizing village defense wherever we had a reliable peasant base. Through a simple system of signals and by synchronizing plans, the local armed nuclei could avoid easy capture and instead inflict losses on any enemy troops that showed up in a village. The effectiveness of such village defense depended on the existence of local nuclei with a solid political background. But all these ideas could be tested only by the reality of war. And this meant risking our lives, because the lives of flesh and blood people were at stake.

By September, after we had evacuated the refugees, there still remained a large number of good combatants in our force. Many who were mere children when we entered the country were now adolescents and had joined our ranks. Many were their fathers, those same nomadic cattle herders who had arrived in the jungle years before carrying only a chest of drawers, a mirror, and a grinding stone, totally unaware of the great changes that were to come into their lives. It was these men who, in the first year of the war, had set out to take over the first village with a flower in the muzzle of their rifles.

FONSECA

Once the mountain guerrilla unit was again up to strength, it took on two tasks that were vital to the organization locally. The first and most urgent was the creation of an infrastructure and a reliable supply system which would give the besieged guerrillas in the jungle an alternative route to the highlands, in case their situation became untenable. The second urgent task, on which the first depended, was to strengthen our organization in the district, which had been badly shaken by the army's offensive. Our successful armed propaganda operation at La Perla made both tasks possible: it consolidated the stalwarts and shook off the waverers.

The secret nuclei we set up at this time came to life in entirely different circumstances. The days of speculating about the future government of the poor and the days when our camp was as busy as a marketplace had long passed. We traveled so silently that only the dogs were occasionally aware of us. In our secret meetings we spoke seriously about the art of conspiracy, the strict selection of new members, and the number of weapons available for waging war. Those new *guerrilleros* who had just learned to read and were still translating the complex concepts of a people's war into their own dialects were assigned to the villages, armed with a revolver and a notebook. There, in their still clumsy writing, they wrote out the basic guidelines for arming the poor with correct ideas and rifles. When the jungle unit arrived in December, the mountain unit was ready to undergo its own first trial by fire.

Fonseca was the most precocious of our organizers in the highlands. He was an Ixil Indian, with light skin, characteristic Indian features, and teeth so small they appeared to be milk teeth. Fonseca had gone to school for a few years, until he had to go to work and contribute to his family's scanty budget. When the time came, he left the schoolroom and joined the men who worked the land. If memory serves, his mother had died, but he had a stepmother who loved him dearly. He migrated to the coast for the first time in his teens and continued doing so every year, because the family's corn crop was always less than enough to feed them.

Fonseca learned to speak Spanish on the coast, and his inquisitiveness grew as he became familiar with the language of capitalist production. From then on, he was possessed by the need to understand the sad reality of his people's hunger and the annual migration to the coast. Once he discovered the guerrillas, he immediately asked to be admitted, and after several months of probation in his village he joined up with the unit in the highlands. There he learned reading and writing, as well as basic math. He spent his spare time practicing his penmanship and copying political articles into his notebook. At study sessions he always asked a thousand questions. In a few months he had grasped the rudiments of the most useful of all sciences, that which teaches people to change the world in a revolutionary way. Enamored of this knowledge, he devoted himself to working toward the realization of an ideal that he had come to understand clearly. But once he went off to organize the villages, he realized how little he actually knew and he began to read in the inexhaustible book of daily life. At eighteen he was already an organizer of a people whose customs were as old as time.

In February 1976, around the time of the earthquake, Fonseca was captured by the enemy in Chajul, a town where *cuta,* or brandy, is made illegally. As in so many highland Indian villages, at fiesta time or at the end of a market day the cobbled streets are strewn with men and women, sleeping off their drunkenness, as though struck down in an invisible war. This vice of colonial origin, alcoholism, is a plague that devastates the highlands, afflicting both men and women at an early age. We did not realize it, but Fonseca had this weakness, fatal to a conspirator who must move in enemy territory. One day while drinking at a bar frequented on market day by strangers and traders he was recognized by a stool pigeon from his home town and reported to the police. Taken on a busy street, he didn't even have time to use his revolver. To make matters worse, he was carrying a compass and a hand grenade in his shoulder bag.

The first round of torture was applied at the Chajul jail. The following night he was taken in an army truck to the command post in San Juan Cotzal. Disfigured and unconscious, he was dumped from the truck as though he were a sack. A young officer immediately began the interrogation, telling Fonseca how young he was and how pointless it was for him to get into this kind of trouble while others went about enjoying life. Then he told him that if he talked he wouldn't be tortured any more.

Meanwhile, the town's secret organization was meeting under an avocado tree and making plans for freeing Fonseca— only to be foiled by the arrival of new truckloads of troops. No rescue operation was possible. Fonseca protected the organization for three days, but on the fourth he blundered: he made up a fantastic story and was trapped in a maze of contradictions. Soon after, he began giving out the names of his *compañeros.* He should never have done that, because from that moment on there was no turning back. As he talked and the enemy officers began to understand the structure of our organization, truckload after truckload of soldiers began to arrive in the area, overrunning the villages and fanning out through the countryside. The roads became dangerous for us to move along. A week later, at a site where the young traitor had trained the first local nucleus, four of its members were caught and executed. After that, Fonseca was seen marching at the head of an enemy column, barefoot, dressed in the enemy's uniform, pointing out houses, roads, and the last sites where we had camped.

We had learned of his capture the day after it happened, however, and had immediately withdrawn. At one site we had hidden a stock of 2,000 pounds of equipment and food. It had taken us several weeks to do this—we dug a cave in the side of a cliff, covered the entrance with a flat stone, placed a piece of plastic over it to keep it dry, and then disguised the hole with pieces of moss. But in the scramble to retreat we failed to cover the plastic carefully and a piece of it was visible. The enemy combed the site and just as they were about to leave—without having discovered anything—one soldier spotted the bright green plastic and notified his commanding officer. They emptied the cave and burned everything. The officer did not even allow his men to take sugar, fearing that it might have been poisoned.

On March 3 the enemy reached our current campsite. It was well hidden in a deep ravine and although we were aware that Fonseca knew of it, we thought it improbable that he would go so far as to lead the enemy there. But we were wrong. One of our patrols sighted the enemy column while walking along a mountain ridge. It was a cold and humid place, covered with lichen and moss. The patrol moved with great caution and could observe the enemy soldiers without being seen: they were just getting up, and some of them, stiff with cold, were basking in the warmth of the early morning sun. They made a lot of noise, and appeared to have no sentry. Our patrol reported immediately to our camp, some 1,500 feet below, after leaving behind a small ambush squad at our usual sentry post. As we prepared to evacuate, the first shots rang out high above us, echoing from peak to peak. A little later, the ambush squad rejoined the main group and made its report. The enemy troop had advanced confidently in single file, frequently falling on the steep and slippery trail. Our ambush squad allowed the soldiers to come so near that when they finally fired they could actually see the equipment in their backpacks and distinguish their faces clearly.

One of the Ixil guerrillas excelled on this occasion: during the rapid initial firing he had advanced without cover, shooting at the astonished soldiers with his carbine. At the first shot the soldiers threw themselves on the ground and were unable to answer the fire until much later, when the ambush squad had already begun to withdraw. During the ensuing skirmish, our men were able to take shelter.

One hour later an army helicopter thundered over the wooded ravine to which we had withdrawn. Later we learned that it was responding to the troop's call for help. Several soldiers were wounded in the ambush, among them a sergeant who was shot in the stomach, and they had immediately informed headquarters of their situation by radio. But the dense vegetation made it difficult for the helicopter to carry out a rescue operation, and the sergeant died while a clearing was being cut so he could be lifted out. His body was flown out the next day, dangling from a cable.

For two months we were isolated from our bases, confined to a virtually uninhabited area. All the surrounding villages and the few inhabited places in the mountains were occupied by the enemy's army. Only isolated houses and the most remote villages escaped this treatment. Troops patrolled the trails and combed the riverbanks in the vicinity of the villages where we had bases. Hundreds of innocent villagers were captured and sent to the military base at Santa Cruz del Quiché. There they were interrogated and subjected to all kinds of torture. The army took whole families, including the children. They questioned them repeatedly about the guerrilla leaders and the local secret nuclei. They stopped anyone they met on the mountain trails or at highway intersections and searched their loads and personal possessions. They even examined the cuffs of men's trousers and split open the tamales people carry to market, looking for messages for the guerrillas. They never found what they were looking for, but six of our collaborators, arrested right after Fonseca turned informer, were executed at the zone's military headquarters. The rest went into hiding and returned the enemy's blows. Two military officers known for terrorizing the local inhabitants were taken by surprise in their house and executed by our village defense group.

Meanwhile, the guerrilla unit in the mountains managed to survive on its food reserves. We did not know what the enemy's tactics would be, and we maintained our vigilance, avoiding the more traveled trails and the large rivers. On the smaller paths near the mountain peaks we would find empty tins and other refuse, clues to the recent whereabouts of the soldiers. The fluttering cry of the flocks of owls flying along the hillsides at dusk would alert us to the enemy's presence. At night, high up on the mountain, we would hear volleys of shots that resounded until they died away among the cliffs and ravines. We were alone in the mountains, the enemy and ourselves.

One month after the ambush in which the sergeant died, the sky above our camp was suddenly filled with a thunderous roar, as though a storm were gathering. A little later we heard explosions in the distance and clearly recognized the sound of aircraft engines. Military jets were bombing the area where the ambush had taken place. We counted sixty-four explosions. A week later the enemy was directly overhead, as a squadron of planes systematically bombed the slopes throughout the mountain zone, dropping fragmentation bombs every hundred yards or so. The first thing we heard was the noise of a plane and the first muffled detonations, similar to rifle shots. Soon the planes were thundering across the ravine and bombs fell into our camp. One fell a few yards from the stream where we bathed. Then the noise became fainter, as the planes moved on. The enemy's objective was apparently to force us to leave the mountains and fight on less favorable terrain.

By April our situation was desperate. Our food was scarce and of poor quality, but we managed to survive by eating wild roots and grasses, wormy corn, and—occasionally—a little good corn that we would get in an isolated settlement. There were weeks in which, due to the amount of roughage we consumed, our excrement resembled the manure of a herbivorous animal. But all that wasn't the main problem. Our worries had to do with the defensive position in which the enemy had placed us. Our communication was cut off by the army's encirclement, while the enemy preyed upon the area's inhabitants. We knew the number of armed combatants was insufficient for us to take the initiative militarily, and thus break the siege and the enemy's offensive. We would have had to win battle after battle if we were to change the situation and put our adversary on the defensive, yet this was clearly impossible given our number and the embryonic nature of the village defense groups. We were still in the process of demonstrating to the population and to our-selves that the guerrilla forces and the local organization could survive an enemy offensive. Our military potential had reached its limit and we had to await the development of other factors. We had to create a more complex strategy in order to deal with the enemy.

The solution arrived by radio. The newscasts were full of reports of the wave of strikes and demonstrations by industrial workers and other groups who were demanding their rights. For the first time in many decades, the language of people's struggle pervaded the mass media and spread to the four winds. The earthquake had shaken Guatemalan society to its very founda-tions and laid bare the corrupt base on which it rested. Risking a clash by crossing enemy lines, we sent our base areas guide-lines on the political struggle that was to be set in motion in the villages. These ideas were compressed into a few pages, but they had the effect of releasing the enormous potential that lay dor-mant among the people. Slowly but increasingly they adopted the guidelines and began to organize protests and make de-mands. Delegations of mothers marched toward the city, de-nouncing to the newspapers and before the urban popular organizations the army's depredations and its policy of genocide among the Ixil population. For the first time the entire country learned that the mountains were being bombed and peasants held captive in rural army garrisons.

In April and May the newscasts were full of military opera-tions. Our urban guerrillas set fire to four trucks loaded with coffee belonging to a land-holding family responsible for re-pression of the highland population of northern Quiché. The burning trucks were a warning to the feudal lords who, using hunting dogs and rifles, overran the villages, capturing any peas-ants who showed signs of rebellion and turning them over to the army. A few days before, in an extraordinarily daring move, our urban organization had attacked a centrally located arsenal and captured arms sufficient for one hundred combatants. A little later a high-ranking intelligence officer was gunned down in the street by guerrillas disguised as itinerant cobblers. Scarcely had the news of this feat been broadcast when there was a report that armed groups of workers on the coast had burned to ashes twenty-two fumigation planes, denouncing the way they poisoned the fields and endangered the health and lives of plantation workers.

The sum total of all these events put the enemy on the defensive across the country. We then prepared to attack the small garrison at Xaxboc. In a week of hard work we collected supplies and reconnoitered the terrain near the garrison. It was an isolated spot in a densely wooded mountain area where the Cuchumatanes descend gently toward the temperate plateau of the Zona Reina, as this area is known. Climbing like goats and marching on mule trails at night, we reached the first houses of the hamlet where the garrison was stationed. A large group of recruits, who were taking up arms for the first time, marched with our column—they had come to our camp the previous week from local village defense groups. Among them was Xan Cam, one of the Ixil leaders we had known during our jungle years. His political life had had many ups and downs ever since then, and he had postponed making the decision to join the guerrillas. This was a common experience for the older people in the Indian regions. Their experience with *ladinos,* who always treated them with contempt and deception, meant that it took a long time for them to accept that our movement could not be for Indians alone but had to be for all poor Guatemalans.

Cam's great intelligence led him to think seriously about these matters since he knew that a commitment on his part meant a commitment for all his followers. He decided that his people's misery and exploitation was the most important consideration, and he took up the cause of those who fought to put an end to these conditions, but who had also helped him to see the link between these and the Indians' condition as a discriminated and oppressed people.

Xan Cam was in the mountains for nineteen months. During that time he developed into a promising organizer, a revolutionary who understood that the guerrilla front in the mountains represented the first line of defense that the Guatemalan Indians would need to fight for their national and social emancipation. In 1978 he got sick and had to go to the city for treatment. His dedication led him to request permission to participate in some of the urban guerrilla operations. Those in charge did not understand the risks implicit in that request and on one of the streets of the capital we lost one of our most promising popular leaders. During the assault on the Colón movie theater—an armed propaganda action involving the urban masses who were, in October of that year, demonstrating and setting up barricades in protest against an increase in the price of public transportation—Xan Cam lagged behind when his *compañeros* withdrew and was surrounded by the police. He fought bravely and protected his departing *compañeros*. Wounded in the legs, he fired his last shots from behind a parked car. At the final moment, he preferred suicide to falling into the enemy's hands.

But all this was after the attack on the Xaxboc garrison. Aside from its tactical importance, this was to be a demonstration of the exemplary methods of the guerrillas, from which the new recruits could learn. However, what it revealed was the lack of thoroughness of our most experienced *compañero*, the man who was responsible for the operation.

At dusk, our large contingent took a row of huts from which the garrison was visible. Instead of using the daylight hours to learn the layout of the installation, the access routes, and the outpost locations, our commander-*compañero*'s attention was diverted by a discussion he had on prices and quantities with a worried local trader who had brought us goods from the remote market in Chajul. He would not accept a lump sum but wanted payment for each item separately—for each small package of crackers and each bottle of soda. We had very few coins, and the operation was complicated as they changed hands again and again. By the time the account was finally settled, it was dark.

At this point two peasants were captured by our advance posts. One of them lived in one of the huts, and had from the outset refused to supply us with any information. Our commander persisted in believing that the man would point out the enemy's outposts to us. The man, however, chose to die instead. We later discovered that he was a civilian spy, working for the army. What followed was a caricature of a military operation. Our column, guided by this captured spy, reached a hilltop from which we should have been able to see the garrison's kerosene lamps, but they could not be distinguished from the lights of the civilian huts. Under these circumstances it was impossible to know what to fire at. The guide, now in handcuffs, still refused to give us any help. Since we had been seen in the village, it would not have been a good idea to postpone the attack until the next day. Our leader therefore presented us with two alternatives: attack the enemy position, trusting to luck, or simply fire at the installation from our present position and then withdraw without trying to make the occupants surrender.

We opted for the latter. There were civilians of all ages in the huts around the garrison and the soldiers took sentry duty in many of them. It would have been patently irresponsible to risk harming the civilians in an attack that ought to have been better prepared that afternoon. So at the order to fire we riddled the garrison with bullets for several minutes, using the light from the street lamps. We then withdrew, leaving behind a complete sample of the various caliber bullets that we were using, as well as the body of the enemy spy. Later we learned that the troops in the garrison, terrified by the sudden burst of gunfire, had quickly disbanded, leaving behind most of their weapons and in some cases even their trousers!

Months later we learned the outcome of Fonseca's story. During the Xaxboc action we heard he had fled from the army, so before going north we left orders that he be tried and shot if he ever tried to contact our organization. The death of so many *compañeros* could not go unpunished; neither could the risky situation in which he had placed our entire organization in that area. When we were back in the jungle we received a tape, in Fonseca's voice, detailing what had happened. They were the words of a man who was already resting forever under the mountain pines. He signed his account "Quetzal," for the bird that cannot live in captivity. His vocabulary now included barracks slang, but in fluent Spanish he told us what had happened after his capture. We relived the recent events in our lives, but this time from the perspective of someone who for months had lived in the confusion and loneliness of the traitor. His love of life had been stronger than his commitment to his country's poor. However, it was an honest confession which made no attempt to deny responsibility.

Fonseca told of how he had been beaten, and of how he had seen the *compañeros* he had betrayed being led to their execution early one morning at the Santa Cruz del Quiché garrison. He told of how he had almost been killed during our ambush on March 3, and of how much he had wanted to run and rejoin his *compañeros,* but fear and confusion had made him freeze, glued to the spot. He told of how the officers, alarmed by the attack, had decided to withdraw immediately and how, together with their troops, they manufactured the stories they would tell their superiors to justify the retreat. He told of how one morning in one of our abandoned camps Rafael—another of the captured men—handcuffed and so badly beaten his features were unrecognizable, had urged him to confess and save Raphael from being further tortured for information he didn't have. During his entire captivity, Fonseca said, he had hoped to escape and return to us—where, in spite of everything, he felt he belonged.

He told us that at no point had the enemy been able to convert him because he had never lost sight of the fact that society is made up of rich and poor, in a life-and-death struggle. Everything they told him only served to confirm this truth. In fact, the soldiers and even some officers recognized it and privately acknowledged that the guerrillas would win sooner or later. Finally, he told us how, at an enemy post near our mountain stronghold, having decided they could trust him, they had given him kitchen duty. One afternoon while the soldiers were playing soccer, he had slipped away into the forest. When they found him gone, the soldiers combed the area, but he managed to reach the isolated hut of one of our collaborators, who hid him, gave him civilian clothing and enough food for one day, and showed him the trail leading out of the area. "You've got to try to be good and not make any more mistakes," said the *compañero* on leaving him.

Some time later Fonseca turned himself in to a local nucleus, ready for whatever punishment would be meted out. He had gone home and his family had offered help and enough money so he could escape to the coast, but he rejected the offer because it would have meant a lifetime of running. When he left to contact the organization, his stepmother told him she had a premonition that she would never see him again. He replied that if he had to die, it should be at the hands of his *compañeros,* since his errors had damaged the organization.

At the moment of his execution, one of the women guerrillas could not hold back her tears. He told her not to weep because his death would serve to keep others from making the same mistakes. At that moment the entire guerrilla unit felt a knot in their throats. In his grave were placed the thirty-two centavos his sisters had sent from his village to accompany him in death.

Listening to Fonseca's tape, we thought about what it means to be a revolutionary. We recalled a faraway bridge back in the highlands where we had once gone to pick up supplies. It was an immensely long and slender tree trunk laid across a dizzying torrent. The endless rain and the turbulent current drenched the trunk, making it glassy-smooth and slippery. We had to cross over twice: to pick up supplies and bring them back—a hundred pounds on our backs. Half-way across, advancing slowly, trying to keep a foothold, the ceaseless flow of the water would suddenly make us feel dizzy. Whoever hesitated at midpoint would become paralyzed, unable to go back or forward. The secret was to cross slowly but without hesitation. We could not have imagined such perils on that night, five years earlier, when we had floated on the gentle current of the Río Lacantún under the January stars, beginning our days of the jungle.